# THE ANDREW McINTOSH PATRICK COLLECTION

To be sold by The Fine Art Society
at 148 New Bond Street · London w1
12 June to 5 July 2007

*Works will not be sold before 6pm
on Tuesday 12 June*

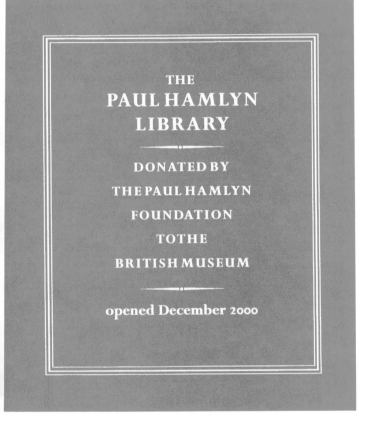

## THE FINE ART SOCIETY

148 New Bond Street · London w1s 2jt
Telephone +44 (0)20 7629 5116
Email art@faslondon.com
Fax +44 (0)20 7491 9454
www. faslondon.com

# The Andrew McIntosh Patrick Collection

THE FINE ART SOCIETY · LONDON 2007

I have found writing this introduction a painful task. It marks the dissolution of a unique collection of art and artefacts assembled over a lifetime by Andrew McIntosh Patrick, one of the most discerning collectors of his age. For those who visited Andrew in his eyrie above The Fine Art Society, or later in his flat near Charing Cross, it will be hard to envisage him apart from the eclectic mix of beautiful objects he had acquired over the last half century: paintings, drawings, prints, sculpture, ceramics, metalwork, furniture, textiles and many other items too numerous to classify here. All were integrated into settings which seemed the embodiment of Andrew himself. Adapting to the loss of this visually enriching experience will not be easy for his friends. Andrew, on the contrary, refreshed by a new challenge, will begin to collect again, perhaps in another country, perhaps in another vein.

The development of Andrew as a collector was intimately entwined with his career at The Fine Art Society (FAS). He joined the FAS straight from his National Service in 1954; in the later 1960s he was appointed Joint Managing Director and in 1975 sole Managing Director, a position he occupied until his retirement in 2004. Alan Powers[1] and Peyton Skipwith[2] (who joined the FAS in 1961) have written informative essays on the period of Andrew's apprenticeship and on his distinctive leadership. The detail of that history will not be repeated here, except to emphasise how, from the mid-1960s onwards, each new recruit brought his own enthusiasms and growing knowledge to the service of the Society. The moribund legacy of the immediate postwar years was soon shaken off. Andrew, as the son of the distinguished Scottish landscape painter James McIntosh Patrick (1907–98), whose paintings had been exhibited at the FAS since the 1930s, brought a personal knowledge of Scottish later nineteenth to twentieth century art to the mix. Equally significant to the future character of the FAS was the enduring influence of the great collectors and scholars Charles and Lavinia Handley-Read. This remarkable couple awakened in Andrew, and in a handful of his contemporaries, a passion for the decorative arts of the past hundred years, for the aesthetic movement, for British sculpture of the pre-First World War period and much else besides. Peyton Skipwith brought his interest in the New English Art Club to the FAS and soon added other fields of expertise including Arts and Crafts English furniture, the Birmingham School and British illustrators. Tony Carroll, who joined the FAS in 1972, developed the exotic connection with groundbreaking exhibitions of artist-travellers in Egypt, Greece and Asia Minor, as well as sparkling shows of stage designs by Leon Bakst. This list offers a mere sample of what was going on at the FAS from the mid-1960s onwards. The exhibition programme was demanding and various. Nearly all the shows explored new aspects of then neglected subjects. Many were loan exhibitions or a mix of loan and sale. Within a decade, Andrew had welded together an organisation within which scholarship, innovation and commerce were equal partners, a distribution of interests which set The Fine Art Society apart from its peers in London and beyond.

My memories of the FAS stretch over fifty years. They sharpen in the late 1960s when a visit to the galleries became an increasingly enriching, though to me a somewhat intimidating, experience. Andrew and Peyton (a dandy in black cape and felt fedora) presided over a space where the decorative arts, furniture, paintings and drawings of the later Victorian and the Edwardian eras jostled hugger-mugger over walls and floors. In 1973 Andrew suggested that a loan exhibition of Sickert's paintings in aid of the Artists' General Benevolent Institution (to coincide with the publication of my first monograph on the artist) be held at both the London and the recently opened Edinburgh galleries of the Society. From then onwards, The Fine Art Society, Andrew and his colleagues became part of my life and above all an essential influence on my visual education.

Andrew's personal collection largely grew in tandem with the exhibition programme of the gallery. I believe this was something of a chicken and egg situation. The exhibitions were inspired by the particular enthusiasms of Andrew and his colleagues and in the process of acquiring, handling and displaying work for exhibition, the need to buy and cherish certain items after the exhibition closed was irresistible.

Despite its eclecticism, Andrew's collection is governed by an identifiable aesthetic. Little dates from before the mid-nineteenth century. There are few very large

paintings or objects. A domestic scale was essential to his display schemes. Pictures were hung in close proximity from dado level to cornice – and when he finally ran out of space on the walls in his flat over The Fine Art Society, he hung black and white prints on the ceiling. Objects – sculpture, metalwork, ceramics – were displayed over every horizontal surface. His ruthless eye demands quality; unless there is some overriding redeeming feature, he is intolerant of imperfections in manufacture, design, handling or composition. His natural inclinations are for muted colour, tonal restraint, smooth brushwork and reticent subject matter. There are naturally exceptions, most strikingly Edward Atkinson Hornel (1864–1933), with his blocky brushwork, crusty surface, hot colours and intricate, agoraphobic design.

Hornel was one of the 'Glasgow Boys', the generation of artists who, during the last quarter of the nineteenth century, revitalised Scottish painting by rejecting academic subjects and style and looking instead for inspiration to the art they had admired during their studies, primarily in France. While the members of this 'school' were sufficiently diverse to invalidate generalisations, it is on the whole true that a primary influence was the *plein-air* naturalism of Jules Bastien-Lepage (1848–84). The Glasgow School forms the kernel of Andrew's collection of paintings. His earliest acquisition was a pastel by James Guthrie, *The Morning Paper* (67), which Andrew fell in love with when it was offered at auction in 1961. His top price was £30. It was bought for £32 by his employers, The Fine Art Society, whose then managing director, in a uniquely generous gesture, agreed to sell it to him at cost (which Andrew managed by borrowing the missing £2 from his mother). In 1967 he bought (again at auction) *St Agnes* (56) an extraordinary image of the virgin martyr standing in contemplation before an extensive landscape, painted *c.*1889 by David Gauld (1865–1936). In its arbitrary dislocation of scale, its two-dimensional pattern of flat, contained colour patches to articulate both figure and landscape backcloth, *St Agnes* not only anticipates Gauld's work as a stained glass designer but presages the stylization of art nouveau. A third early acquisition, and a star of his collection, was *Stirling Station* of *c.*1888 by William Kennedy (1859–1918; 81). He had spotted it in 1968, when it was exhibited at Glasgow Art Gallery in the first major exhibition of the group. The private owner had just given it to her daughter who was willing to sell at a price Andrew

could not then afford. He bought it. In 1970, the FAS introduced London to *The Glasgow School of Painting*, through a loan exhibition which included *St Agnes* and *Stirling Station*. Most of the artists represented were to find a secure place in Andrew's collection. He acquired three views of Grèz-sur-Loing outside Paris where, emulating the habit common among nineteenth-century French painters of working alongside each other at a particular place, several of the Glasgow artists congregated: *A Grey Summer's Day, Grèz* by John Lavery (1856–1941); *Les Laveuses, Grèz* by Arthur Melville (1855–1904) from Charles Handley-Read's collection, given to Andrew in 1971 by Lavinia Handley-Read, his widow; and a view of Grèz by Gauld. His selection was remarkable for its foresight as well as for its aesthetic quality. In 1999, when Andrew moved from his flat over The Fine Art Society and needed to raise the money to buy a flat elsewhere, the National Gallery of Scotland saw its chance to fill a void in its own holdings. A private treaty sale was negotiated of three of Andrew's finest 'Glasgow Boy' paintings: Gauld's *St Agnes*, *Miss Sowerby* of 1882, an exquisite profile portrait of a standing girl by James Guthrie (1859–1930) which had been included in the 1970 FAS exhibition, and *A Daydream* of 1885 by E. A. Walton (1860–1922), showing a young girl seated in a landscape, her eyes glazed, her thoughts far away.

A plasticine relief by Joseph Crawhall (1821–96; 39) combines Andrew's passion for the 'Glasgow Boys' with his more quirky love of camels. His camel collection inludes three small bronze sculptures by Antoine-Louis Barye (1795–1875), the noted French *animalier*: a *Small Persian Camel*, an *Algerian Dromedary* and one plain, undifferentiated *Camel*; two camel bronzes by Edward Onslow Ford (1852–1901), one with General Gordon aboard; and camels feature in many of his watercolours and drawings of the deserts, markets and bedouin camps of north Africa, some by nineteenth century travellers such as Edwin Alexander (1870–1926), Thomas Seddon (1821–56) and Edward Lear (1812–88), and some by contemporary artists such as the Scottish illustrator and wild-life painter Keith Brockie (b.1955) .

Andrew's fascination with camels developed hand in hand with the innovative exhibitions held at The Fine Art Society in the 1970s which explored artist travellers in the eastern Mediterranean and North Africa during the nineteenth century. He first saw one of the most striking watercolours in his collection, *Lieutenant Richard Burton in Arab Dress standing by a seated Camel in the Desert* of 1851 by Thomas Seddon (137), when it was included in (and illustrated on the catalogue cover of) the earliest of these exhibitions, *North African Traveller: Casablanca to Cairo* in 1974. He never forgot it and was able to buy it some ten years later. Several other works featuring camels in the same exhibition were to enter his collection, including Edwin Alexander's *Camel at the Artist's Camp with the Bedouins* (2), his Joseph Crawhall plasticine relief and his bronze *Camel* by Edward Onslow Ford. *North African Traveller* was devoted exclusively to British artists, a high proportion of them Scottish. In 1978, the FAS organised a more ambitious exhibition, incorporating Continental as well as British artists, under the title *Eastern Encounters: Orientalist Painters of the Nineteenth Century*. Some fifteen years later Andrew was to acquire a version of a highlight of the 1978 exhibition, Seddon's *Dromedary and Arabs at the City of the Dead, Cairo*.

From its first years, The Fine Art Society had welcomed exhibitions of work done by European artists in exotic lands: views of India and Kashmir, Constantinople and Egypt were often to be found on show in the gallery from 1876 onwards. In 1890 the Society had showed *Pictures and Drawings of the Landscape of Japan* by Alfred East (1844–1913). In 1976, the Society decided to celebrate its centenary with 'FAS 100', an exhibition which reintroduced the key themes explored during one hundred years of trade at 148 New Bond Street. Three views of Japan by East (one, *Dawn on the Sacred Mountain*, from the artist's 1890 exhibition) were included. Another, a distant view of Fujiyama painted in oil on panel, is similar in scale and subject to a painting by East which Andrew was to acquire (48), together with a watercolour by Mortimer Menpes (1855–1938) of *Buildings by a River, Japan*, in 1991 (121) when he organised *Opening the Window – British Artists in Meiji Japan*, an exhibition devoted to the art of East and Menpes.

Andrew's purchase, in 1977, of Hornel's *Japanese Figures in a Garden* (76) painted in Tokyo in 1896, drew together two of his chief interests as a collector, 'The Glasgow Boys' and Japan. Many of the Glasgow artists travelled to warmer and more colourful lands. George Henry as well as Hornel travelled to Japan. Lavery and Crawhall passed much of their time in Morocco. Melville spent two adventurous years between 1880 and 1882

travelling in the Middle East, India and Asia Minor as well as visiting Spain, Tangiers and Algeria in the 1890s. Andrew's collection of work by Melville, all acquired direct from Marian Melville, the artist's daughter, ranges from the early tender oil painting *The Cabbage Garden* (120) to watercolours such as *El Primo, Madrid* and *The Bazaar at Vringa*, spectacular examples of how Melville applied bold colour directly, with no underlying drawing, onto wet paper.

The Fine Art Society had been quick to support the fashion for the decorative arts of Japan. In 1888 and 1893, the Society exhibited a wide selection of Japanese artefacts, including ceramics, metal and lacquer work; Japanese dolls were exhibited in 1909, fans in 1914. The FAS had also staged major exhibitions of Japanese prints, including the first showing outside Japan of Hokusai drawings and engravings (1890), a survey of outstanding prints from the primitives to Hiroshige (1909) and Hiroshige alone (1914). The connection between the FAS and Japan was memorably revived in 1972 with *The Aesthetic Movement and the Cult of Japan*. This exhibition established the unique character of the FAS over the next forty years by reasserting that the decorative arts not only deserved attention from scholars but were magnificently rewarding visually. Inspired by Charles Handley-Read who had died the year before it opened, the show was organised by Andrew with the help of other Handley-Read disciples, notably Michael Whiteway and Stuart Durrant (the FAS was henceforth to collaborate with Whiteway in many further exhibitions devoted to the decorative arts). Andrew masterminded the display.

Andrew's genius (there is no other word for it) for arranging objects to stunning visual effect was crucial not only to the gallery, but also to the display of his personal collection. To see him arrange two strips of Japanese textiles on a taut bedcover, adjust the relationship of a porcelain bowl and a bronze lamp on a table, closely hang the walls of an anteroom with Ukioy-e prints, was a revelation. He acquired Japanese and Asian artefacts, ancient and modern, sporadically, over the years of working and travelling for the FAS. His furniture, all in everyday use, includes pieces by the greatest designers of the nineteenth century, for example Augustus Welby Pugin (1812–52), Charles Rennie Mackintosh (1868–1928), William Morris (1834–96) and E. W. Godwin (1833–86).[3] He also has choice pieces of twentieth century furniture, notably a versatile oak bookcase and a laminated birch dinner wagon both designed by Gerald Summers (1899–1967) in the 1930s for Makers of

Simple Furniture, and a side chair in bent plywood by Basil Spence (1907–76). He has lamps and chafing dishes and candleholders by W. A. S. Benson (1854–1924), hearthside items – fenders, firedogs and ash pans by Thomas Jeckyll (1827–81). However, his most focussed activity as a decorative arts collector was devoted to the work of Dr Christopher Dresser (1834–1904).

In terms of quality and scholarship, with each piece thoroughly researched and understood in context, Andrew's was by far the most significant and comprehensive private collection of Dresser's work ever assembled. Again it was Charles Handley-Read who pioneered the study of Dresser. Thus, alongside *The Aesthetic Movement* exhibition held at the FAS in 1972, John Jesse and Richard Dennis, two more Handley-Read disciples, were given the use of the upper floor gallery to mount the first comprehensive exhibition of Dresser's work as designer of pottery, glass and metal work. Besides an extensive representation of Dresser's pottery and glass, Andrew's personal collection also incorporates furniture, textiles, even a picnic set designed by Dresser. His Dresser metal work collection, most of it now sold, included teapots, sugars, creamers, toast racks, claret jugs, condiment sets, bottles and baskets. Happily, the Victoria and Albert Museum acquired two of the most spectacular teapots by private treaty sale, one a tipped-up square silver-plate and ebony pot manufactured by James Dixon of Sheffield c.1879, the other an exquisite silver, bone and enamel pot manufactured in Birmingham of 1878. Andrew gave the Museum his hemispherical silver plate teapot, also manufactured by Dixon.

It is impossible in this introduction to do more than touch on themes within Andrew's collection. A visit to his flat was to enter an Aladdin's cave where the eye hardly knew where to begin and where his warm hospitality soon distracted attention from close study. One of the curiosities was how well-integrated were his decorative arts objects, often flamboyant in style, and his wall-hung pictures, usually restrained in mood and handling. Among my favourites is his choice selection of paintings by Paul Maitland (1860–1909), delicate views in muted tones and colours of Battersea, Kensington Gardens and Rochester Harbour. In 1969, *This Earthly Paradise*, an exhibition at the Society of works by the then forgotten 'Birmingham School', brought Maxwell Armfield (1882–1972), the only surviving member of the school, into contact with the FAS. Armfield had been closely associated with the revival of

tempera painting in Birmingham at the beginning of the century. His work immediately appealed to Andrew and his colleagues. The exhibition *Homage to Maxwell Armfield* followed in 1970, a 90th Birthday show in 1971, a memorial show in 1973 and 'Flower Studies' in 1977. Andrew himself acquired several works by Armfield, watercolours, paintings in tempera, as well as *Camel in Moonlight*, a drawing of a camel on black paper.

Among the many contemporary artists and craftsmen collected by Andrew are Harriet Mena Hill (b.1966), Philip Reeves (b.1931) and Eileen Hogan (b.1946). All have had exhibitions at The Fine Art Society. Hill uses tempera on gesso to paint, often on found objects, intricate, enclosed spaces. Reeves, English-born but Scottish by adoption, creates spare, abstract collages. Hogan paints places, mostly in London but occasionally abroad, using oil or watercolour with a delicate touch to evoke a sharp sense of atmosphere. The quality which unites these three artists is cool elegance. Leonard Rosoman (b.1913) is represented by works which have a personal resonance, including a watercolour of a corner of The Fine Art Society and a gouache related to the magnificent portrait he painted of Andrew at The Fine Art Society in 1987.

This resumé risks descent into a catalogue of names and titles which do no justice to the collection they describe. However, I cannot end without citing one more painting which I will forever associate with Andrew. I saw it when first I went into the kitchen of his flat above the gallery in 1973. It is a small watercolour by Mariano Fortuny y Madrazo (1838–1874, best-remembered today for being the father of the famous dress and fabric designer) of a gracefully poised *Marabou Stork*, fragile and elusive [frontispiece]. This picture encapsulates, for me, the sense in which Andrew's innate collecting instinct is driven by his love of beautiful things. Wherever his future lies, I am certain that he will again accumulate objects of beauty. He cannot help himself. ✺

1. 'The Fine Art Society 1914–2001', introductory essay to
*The Fine Art Society Story*, Part 2, (2001) pp 4–15, the second of two exhibition catalogues celebrating the first 125 years of the Society.
2. 'The Fine Art Society 1954–2004: A Fifty Year Survey', FAS NOW, (Spring 2007).
3. In 1881 Godwin redesigned the handsome façade of The Fine Art Society and the deep vestibule with display showcase windows which survive, largely intact, to this day.

*Part One · Paintings, Sculpture & Works on Paper*

**1**

EDWIN JOHN ALEXANDER RSA RSW
1870–1926

*Head of a Camel*, 1889

Pen and ink on paper, signed and dated *February 1889*
6¾ × 6 inches (17 × 15 cm)

**2**

EDWIN JOHN ALEXANDER RSA RSW
1870–1926

*Camel at the Artist's Camp with the Bedouins*

Watercolour on paper, signed with initials lower left
12⅜ × 21¼ inches (31.5 × 53 cm)

**3**

EDWIN JOHN ALEXANDER RSA RSW
1870–1926

*Smoke in the Desert*, 1914

Gouache and watercolour on linen, signed and dated
20 × 30 inches (49 × 73 cm)

**4**

ROBERT ALEXANDER RSA
1840–1923

*Donkeys at Blackheath*, 1874

Oil on board, signed and dated lower left
7 × 9½ inches (17.8 × 24.2 cm)

5

MAXWELL ASHBY ARMFIELD
1881–1972
*Self Portrait*

Tempera on panel, signed with monogram lower left, inscribed verso
'based on a study made 1902'
5½ × 5½ inches (14 × 14 cm)
PROVENANCE: Alexander Ballard
EXHIBITED: Southampton Art Gallery, *Maxwell Armfield*, 1978 (84)

6

MAXWELL ASHBY ARMFIELD
1881–1972
*Miniature portrait of Harley Granville-Barker*, 1900

Tempera, signed MA | MDCCC lower left
2½ × 1¾ inches (6.4 × 4.5 cm)

Harley Granville-Barker (1871–1946) was an English actor,
director, producer, critic and playwright. He made his first stage appearance at
the age of 14 and became a leading member of the Stage Society in
1900: this led to contact with George Bernard Shaw. Granville-
Barker took a lease on the Royal Court Theatre and among many of
the works he produced were plays by Shaw, Ibsen and Maeterlinck.
His best-known plays are *The Voysey Inheritance*, *Waste* and *The
Madras House*.

7

MAXWELL ASHBY ARMFIELD
1881–1972
*New Roses, carpet design*, 1935

Pencil, gouache and watercolour, signed with monogram
11¾ × 8⅝ inches (30 × 22 cm)
PROVENANCE: Alexander Ballard; The Laporte Corporate
Art Collection
EXHIBITED: Raeburn Gallery, 1935; Southampton &
Birmingham Art Galleries, 1978
LITERATURE: *Homage to Maxwell Armfield*, FAS cat, 1970;
Laporte, *A History in Art*, 2000 (2–6)

8

MAXWELL ASHBY ARMFIELD
1881–1972

*Worcester Martelet, Carpet Design*, 1935

Pencil, gouache and watercolour, signed with monogram
11¾ × 8⅝ inches (30 × 22 cm)
PROVENANCE: Alexander Ballard
EXHIBITED: Raeburn Gallery, 1935; Southampton and
Birmingham Art Galleries 1978

9

MAXWELL ASHBY ARMFIELD
1881–1972

*Weeds*, 1905

Watercolour
3⅛ × 4⅛ inches (8 × 10.4 cm)
PROVENANCE: Alexander Ballard

10

MAXWELL ASHBY ARMFIELD
1881–1972

*Keith Henderson, c.*1902

Tempera on board, signed with monogram lower right
6½ × 6⅝ inches (16.5 × 16.8 cm)
EXHIBITED: London, The Fine Art Society, *Homage to
Maxwell Armfield*, 1970 (18)

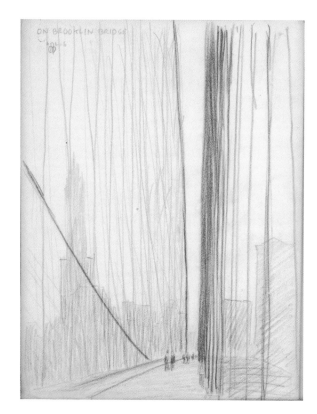

**11**

MAXWELL ASHBY ARMFIELD
1881–1972

*On Brooklyn Bridge*, 1916

Coloured chalks, signed with monogram,
inscribed with title and dated *6.6.16* upper left
10½ × 8 inches (26.7 × 20.3 cm)

**12**

MAXWELL ASHBY ARMFIELD
1881–1972

*Exotic miniature, c.1969*

Tempera, signed with monogram lower right
5¾ × 6 inches (14.7 × 15.2 cm)

**13**

JAMES BAMBOROUGH
FL. 1865–1885

*The Friendly Critic*, 1866

Watercolour
8¾ × 6¾ inches (22.3 × 17.3 cm)
EXHIBITED: Edinburgh, Royal Scottish Academy, 1866 (213)

## 14

EDWARD BAWDEN CBE RA
1903–1989

*Design for an Endpaper for The Story of Rasselas, c.1979*

Pen and watercolour over pencil on paper, inscribed *Rasselas* lower left
and *Cover (sketch)* lower centre and signed *Edward Bawden*, lower right
9½ × 5¾ inches (24.2 × 14.7 cm)
LITERATURE: Edward Bawden and Douglas Percy Bliss *The History of
Rasselas, Prince of Abyssinia*, The Pendomer Press, 1979

## 15

GILBERT WILLIAM BAYES RA
1872–1953

*The Knight Errant, 1913*

Bronze, parcel gilt, inscribed *Gilbert Bayes 1913*, around the base; on
original ebonised stand · 9 inches (23 cm) stand 52 inches (132 cm)
PROVENANCE: Charles and Lavinia Handley-Read
EXHIBITED: London, Royal Academy of Arts, *Victorian and Edwardian
Decorative Art: The Handley-Read Collection*, 1972 (F6) p105

## 16

ROBERT ANNING BELL RA RWS NEAC
1873–1933

*Lady of the Fountain, 1905*

Oil on panel · 5½ × 6¾ inches (14 × 17.2 cm)

## 17

MANUEL BENEDITO-VIVES
1875–1963

*The Beach Comber*

Gouache · 2 × 2¼ inches (5 × 5.7 cm)

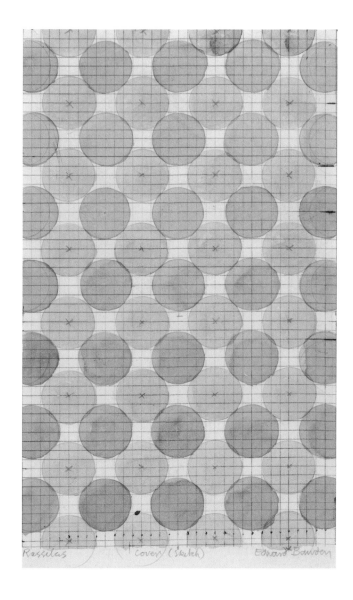

## 18

JEFFREY BLONDES
BORN 1956
*Les Moulins des Roches V*, 1997

Etching, numbered 20 from an edition of 25
4 × 10 inches (10.2 × 25.3 cm)

## 19

JEFFREY BLONDES
BORN 1956
*L'Heraudière III*, 1995

Oil on board
7½ × 10¼ inches (19 × 26 cm)
EXHIBITED: London, The Fine Art Society, *Jeffrey Blondes* 1996 (11)

20

## 20

GUY PENE DU BOIS
1884–1958
*Nocturne, Paris*, 1905

Oil on panel, signed *Guy du Bois '05*, lower right
9½ × 13 inches (24.2 × 33 cm)
EXHIBITED: London, The Fine Art Society *Spring* 1990 (30)

## 21

SIR MUIRHEAD BONE
1876–1953
*From an Adelphi Flat – Charing Cross*, c.1905

Drawing in pencil on white wove paper, signed in pencil *Muirhead Bone*, lower right centre
7 × 10 inches (17.7 × 25.1 cm)

21

## 22

SIR MUIRHEAD BONE
1876–1953
*The Bargello and Badia, Florence*, 1911

Drypoint, signed in pencil *Muirhead Bone*, lower right: one of only four impressions
13½ × 7¾ inches (34.2 × 19.5 cm)
REFERENCE: Campbell Dodgson 274

## 23

CHRISTOPHER BRAMHAM
BORN 1952
*Pen Ponds, Richmond, February*, 1988

Pastel on paper, signed lower right
9 × 13 inches (22.8 × 33 cm)
EXHIBITED: London, The Fine Art Society, 1988 (39)

23

## 24

GERALD LESLIE BROCKHURST RA
1890–1978

*Seule*, 1923

Etching, signed in pencil *G.L. Brockhurst*, lower right, printed in black ink on wove paper: a proof in the first state, before the reduction of the plate and the edition of 76

6 × 7⅞ inches (15.2 × 20.1 cm)

REFERENCE: Wright 36 i | IV

## 25

GERALD LESLIE BROCKHURST RA
1890–1978

*Cypriano*, 1927

Etching, signed in pencil *G.L. Brockhurst*, lower right, printed in black ink on wove paper: from the edition of 111

REFERENCE: Wright 59

6⅜ × 3¾ inches (16.2 × 9.5 cm)

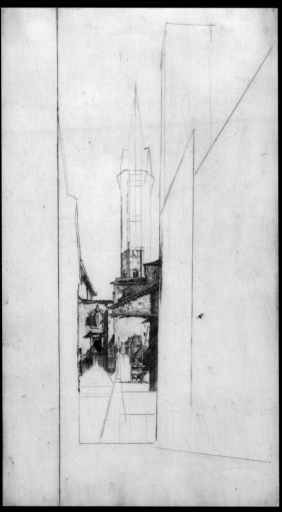

22

**26**

ROBERT BROUGH
1872–1905
*Study for Victoria Bridge, Aberdeen*

Oil on board, signed in pencil lower right
6 × 9 inches (15.2 × 22.8 cm)
EXHIBITED: Aberdeen Art Gallery, *Robert Brough* 1995 (32)

**27**

ROBERT BROUGH
1872–1905
*The Dornoch Train, c.1900*

Oil on panel, inscribed 'To Ned'
10½ × 13½ inches (26.7 × 34.3 cm)
EXHIBITED: Aberdeen Art Gallery, *Robert Brough* 1995 (27)

28

WILLIAM LEENDERT BRUCKMAN
1866–1928

*The Steam Train*

Oil on panel, signed, *W L Bruckman*, lower right
8¾ × 10¾ inches (22.2 × 27.3 cm)

32

## 29

WINIFRED MABEL BRUNTON
1880–1959
*West Wall of the Shrine of Amen, Abydos*

Watercolour heightened with white, initialled lower left *W.M.N.B*
5 × 3 inches (12.7 × 7.6 cm)

## 30

SIR DAVID YOUNG CAMERON RA
1865–1945
*The Three Barrows, 1891*

Etching, signed in pencil *D.Y. Cameron,* lower right, printed in black
on laid paper, one of about 6 impressions recorded by Rinder, who
describes it as a London subject · 1 × 6¾ inches (2.5 × 16.1 cm)
EXHIBITED: Scottish Arts Council, *With an Eye to the East,* 1988
REFERENCE: Rinder 82

## 31

SIR DAVID YOUNG CAMERON RA
1865–1945
*The Steps, 1892*

Etching, signed in pencil *D.Y. Cameron,* lower right, printed in black
on wove paper · 10 × 3 inches (25.3 × 7.5 cm)
EXHIBITED: Scottish Arts Council, *With an Eye to the East,* 1988
REFERENCE: Rinder 113

## 32

MARTIN CHURCHILL
BORN 1954
*Kinnaird House, 2003*

Oil on board, signed *Churchill* and dated *'03* lower right
12 × 18 inches (30.5 x45.8 cm)

## 33

MARTIN CHURCHILL
BORN 1954
*The Scottish Carpet House, 1985*

Oil on panel · 20½ × 28½ inches (52 × 72.5 cm)

**34**

ITHELL COLQUHOUN
1906–1988
*Flowers in a Yellow Vase*, 1962

Oil on panel, signed with monogram, lower left
13¼ × 9¼ inches (33.5 × 23.5 cm)

**35**

IRENE CODREANO
1897–1985
*A Thai Girl*, 1927

Bronze on ebonised base
9½ inches (24 cm) high

**36**

EDWARD GORDON CRAIG
1872–1966
*Descending into the Tomb*, 1907

Etching, signed in pencil with initials EGC and dated 1907, trimmed by the artist around the platemark, leaving a signature tab: one of the subjects published by the artist in *A Portfolio of Etchings*, 1908; 12 of the intended 30 sets were completed
8 × 6½ inches (20.4 × 16.4 cm)

**37**

JOSEPH CRAWHALL RSW
1861–1913
*James Guthrie at his Easel*, 1885

Oil on panel
6 × 8 inches (15.2 × 20.3 cm)

## 38

JOSEPH CRAWHALL RSW
1861–1913
*A Tethered Camel, c.1898*

Plasticine relief · 8⅜ × 7¼ × 1¼ inches (22 × 18.5 × 3.2 cm)

Adrian Bury mentions two sculptures by Crawhall: bronze bas-reliefs of a camel and an ibex. There were casts of the camel, the size of which corresponds to our plasticine relief, in the collections of Pierre Jeannerat and A.C.J. Wall, cited in Adrian Bury, *Joseph Crawhall, the Man and the Artist*, London 1958, p.242. This relief sculpture must date from after his Tangier years as the material, Plasticine, was formulated by art teacher William Harbutt of Bathampton, near Bath, England in 1897. He wanted a non-drying clay for use by his students. The original Plasticine was grey.
*We are grateful to Sir Peter Blake RA for his assistance in preparing this entry.*

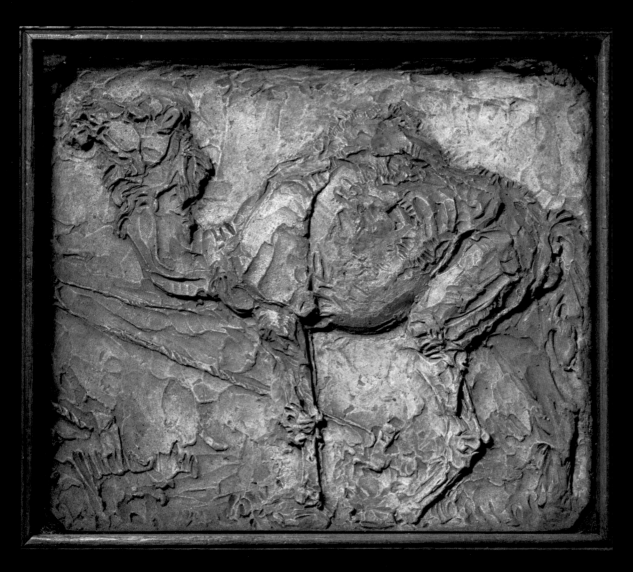

39

THOMAS HARTLEY CROMEK
1809–1873
*Two Camels*

Watercolour, inscribed *Athens, 24 August 18?4*, lower left
5½ × 8¼ inches (14 × 21 cm)

40

EDGAR DEGAS
1834–1917
*Ludovic Halevy Dans les Coulisses c.1880–3*

Monotype, with the stamped signature
9⅝ × 6¼ inches (24.5 × 15.8 cm)
This monotype is an illustration for Ludovic Halevy's 1878 novel,
*Ludovic Halevy dans les Coulisses Famille Cardinal*
PROVENANCE: Atelier Degas, 22 & 23 Nov 1918, part of lot 201, Marcel
Guerin; Mme Huguette Beres
LITERATURE: Janis E. Parry, *Degas Monotypes. Essay, Catalogue and
Checklist*, Fogg Art Museum, 1968, (224); Jean Adhemar & Francoise
Cashin, *Degas Gravures et Monotypes*, Paris 1972 (70)

41

JOHN DODGSON
1890–1969
*Christmas Card*, 1957

6 × 7½ inches (15.2 × 19 cm)
EXHIBITED: Ipswich, Christchurch Mansion, 1997

42

SIR WILLIAM FETTES DOUGLAS PRSA RSW
1822–1891
*The Bass Rock* 1880

Oil on board · 4¾ × 12½ inches (12 × 31.8 cm)

43

THOMAS MILLIE DOW
1848–1919
*Trees*, 1886

Oil on canvas, signed and dated lower left
36 × 30 inches (91.5 × 76 cm)

## 44

LOUIS DUPRÉ
1789–1837

*Repas du Gouverneur ou Voyage d'Athènes d'Aprés nature en*, 1819

Coloured lithograph, signed in pencil *L Dupre*, lower right
6 × 8 inches (15.2 × 20.3 cm)

## 45

LOUIS DUPRÉ
1789–1837

*Ishmael Bey et Mahemet Pasha Filles de Veli Pacha de Thessalie et Petit-Fils de Ali Tebelen, Visir de Janina*

Hand coloured lithograph, signed in pencil *L Dupre*, lower left
11 × 16¼ inches (28 × 41.3 cm)
EXHIBITED: London, The Fine Art Society, *Travellers Beyond the Grand Tour*, 1980 (L1)

## 46

LOUIS DUPRÉ
1789–1837

*Le Palais et le Fortresse de Janina, Vus du Lac: Un Turc et Un Jeune Grec*

Hand coloured lithograph, signed lower right
11½ × 16¼ inches
(28 × 41.3 cm)
EXHIBITED: London, The Fine Art Society, *A Journey through Greece*, 1981

## 47

JOSEPH DURHAM
1814–1877
*The Rowers*, 1866

Bronze
18 inches (46 cm)

## 48

SIR ALFRED EAST RA
1849–1913

*New Moon and Rain Showers
– A View of Kara-Saki from
the South-East, c.*1890

Oil on panel, signed *Alfred East*,
lower left and with 'inkan' (Alfred
East phonetically) · 9¼ × 6 inches
(23.5 × 15.2 cm)
EXHIBITED: London, The Fine Art
Society *The Landscape of Japan* 1890
(61); Edinburgh and London, The
Fine Art Society, *Opening the
Window*, 1991 (11)
East was commissioned by The Fine
Art Society to travel to Japan for six
months in 1889, and the exhibition
of the resulting works in 1890 led
to much acclaim.

**49**

JOHN FAED RSA
1819–1902
*Mill on the Fleet, Gatehouse of Fleet*

Oil on canvas
13½ × 18½ inches (34.3 × 47 cm)
EXHIBITED: (possibly) RSA 1861 (268); Kirkcudbright, *John Faed Centenary Exhibition*, 2002 (41)

This is a view of the Gatehouse of Fleet from the artist's house, Ardmore.

**50**

JOHN FAED RSA
1819–1902
*Sir Joshua Reynolds and Dr Samuel Johnson*,
1870

Oil on canvas, laid on board
5½ × 5 inches (14 × 12.7 cm)

### 51

JAMES FAIRGRIEVE RSA
BORN 1944
*Maes Howe, Orkney*

Oil on board · 7 × 7 inches (17.8 × 17.8 cm)

### 52

MARIANO FORTUNY Y MADRAZO
1838–1874
*A Marabou Stork*

Ink and watercolour, with the studio stamp lower left
11½ × 7½ inches (29.3 × 19 cm)

This painter was the father of the renowned textile and fashion designer.

*Illustrated opposite title page*

### 53

LOUIS RICHARD GARBE
1876–1957
*A Song to Passing Summer*, 1902

Ivory low relief with metal, inscribed *Richard Garbe 1902*
13 inches (33 cm) high 7 inches (17.7 cm) wide
PROVENANCE: Charles and Lavinia Handley-Read
EXHIBITED: London, Royal Academy of Arts 1902
(1679); London, Royal Academy of Arts *Victorian and Edwardian Decorative Art: The Handley-Read Collection*, 1972 (F17), p107; Brighton, Museum and Art Gallery *Beauty's Awakening: The Centenary Exhibition of the Art Workers' Guild*, 1984 (165)

**54**

DAVID GAULD RSA
1865–1936
*The Procession of St Agnes – Stained Glass Design c.1890–93*

Watercolour and pencil on paper
4½ × 4 inches (11.4 × 10.2 cm)
PROVENANCE: Martin Harrison
LITERATURE: Roger Billcliffe, *The Glasgow Boys*, London 1985 pp.265–7

**55**

DAVID GAULD RSA
1865–1936
*The Procession of St Agnes – Stained Glass Design, c.1890–93*

Watercolour and pencil on paper
4½ × 4 inches (11.4 × 10.2 cm)
PROVENANCE: Martin Harrison
LITERATURE: Roger Billcliffe, *The Glasgow Boys*, London 1985 pp.265–7

**56**

DAVID GAULD RSA
1865–1936
*Grez from the River, c.1896*

Oil on canvas, signed and dated lower left
20 × 24 inches (50.8 × 61 cm)
EXHIBITED: London, Barbican Art Gallery *Impressionism in Britain* 1995 (83)
LITERATURE: Roger Billcliffe, *The Glasgow Boys*, London 1985 p.267 no.247

57

DAVID GAULD RSA
1865–1936
*The Procession of St Agnes*
Watercolour · 17 × 16½ inches (43.2 × 41.8 cm)

**58**

JEAN-LÉON GÉRÔME
1824–1904

*Arnauts Fumant*, 1896

Etching, printed in black ink on paper
6⅝ × 9⅜ inches (16.8 × 23.8 cm)

**59**

GLUCK
1895–1978

*Edith Craig in Uniform, c.*1940

Oil on canvas
4¾ × 6¾ inches (12.2 × 17.3 cm)

**60**

GLUCK
1895–1978

*Judge Green*

Oil on panel
3 × 2½ inches (7.7 × 6.3 cm)

61

THOMAS COOPER GOTCH
1854–1931
*Contre-Jour – Peeling the Vegetables*
Pastel · 6¾ × 4½ inches (17.2 × 11.4 cm)

62

THOMAS COOPER GOTCH
1854–1931
*Penzance Harbour, c.1887*
Watercolour, signed *T.C. Gotch*, lower left, and inscribed *to my friend Alfred East* · 13½ × 17½ inches (34.3 × 44.3 cm)

63

WALTER GREAVES
1846–1930
*The Aquatic Tavern*

Oil on canvas
21 × 17 inches (53.2 × 43.2 cm)
PROVENANCE: The Estate of Amaryllis Fleming
EXHIBITED: London, The Fine Art Society *The Fine Art Society Story, Part 1* 2001 (65)

The Aquatic Tavern was next door to J.M.W. Turner's retreat, where he lived with the widowed Mrs Booth, the building now replaced by 119 Cheyne Row. It was near the wharves and creek that separated Chelsea from Fulham.

64

MAURICE GREIFFENHAGEN
1862–1931

*Woman with a Japanese Fan*, 1885

Oil on canvas, signed and dated upper left
7 × 10 inches (17.8 × 25.4 cm)
EXHIBITED: London, Barbican Art Gallery and Tokyo,
Setagaya Art Museum, *Japan and Britain: An Aesthetic
Dialogue 1850–1930* 1991 (92)
LITERATURE: Tomoko Sato and Toshio Watanabe (ed),
*Japan and Britain: An Aesthetic Dialogue 1850–1930*
London 1991 p112, illustrated

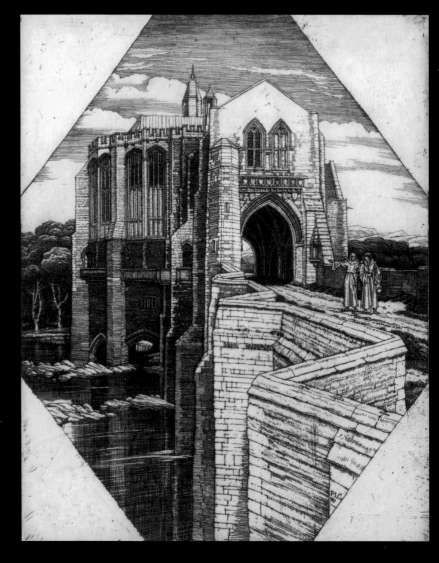

## 65

FREDERICK GRIGGS RA
1876–1938
*Palace Court*, 1933

Etching, signed in pencil *F.L. Griggs*, lower right, printed in
black ink on laid paper, trimmed to narrow margins by the
artist: one of 75 impressions in the third (final) state
10 × 7 inches (25.5 × 17.8 cm)
REFERENCE: Comstock 49 iii | III

## 66

FREDERICK GRIGGS RA
1876–1938
*St Botolph's Bridge no.2*, 1936

Etching, signed in pencil *F.L. Griggs*, lower right and dated *29 Ap*,
lower left, printed in black ink on wove paper, one of an unrecorded
edition in the third state (of four)
9¾ × 7⅞ inches (25 × 20 cm)
REFERENCE: Comstock 56 iii | IV

SIR JAMES GUTHRIE RA PRSA
1859–1930
*The Morning Paper*, 1890

Pastel, signed and dated *J. Guthrie 90*, lower left
19 × 24 inches (48.2 × 61 cm)
PROVENANCE: Captain J.M.S. Steuart, Strathtay
EXHIBITED: Glasgow, Lawrie's Gallery *Exhibition of
Pastels* 1891; Edinburgh, The Royal Scottish Academy
*Guthrie Memorial Exhibition* 1931; Arts Council
Touring Exhibition, *Decade 1890–1900*, 1967 (72);
London, The Fine Art Society, *The Glasgow School of
Painting* 1970 (11); Helensburgh, *Helensburgh and the
Glasgow School* 1972 (12)
LITERATURE: Sir James L. Caw, *Sir James Guthrie:
a biography* London 1932 p234

**68**

SIR JAMES GUTHRIE RA PRSA
1859–1930

*The Shepherd Boy, c.1881*

Oil on canvas, signed lower right
39 × 16 inches (99 × 40.6 cm)
EXHIBITED: Glasgow, The Fine Art Society *Guthrie and the Scottish Realists* 1981 (21)
LITERATURE: Roger Billcliffe, *The Glasgow Boys* London 1985 p.56
Possibly a design for a stained glass window in a house at Kilcreggan, Argyll of 1887

**69**

JAMES J GUTHRIE
1874–1952

*Harting, Peartree Press*

Pastel, watercolour and ink on prepared board
7½ × 11¾ (19 × 30 cm)

**70**

CARL HAAG
1820–1915

*The Ruins of Ancient Tiberius, 1859*

Watercolour, signed and dated lower right, inscribed *The Ruins of Ancient Tiberius* lower left
6½ × 19¼ inches (16.5 × 49 cm)

**71**

GEORGE EDWARDS HERING
1805–1879

*Standing Stones on Machrie Moor, Isle of Arran, 1861*

Oil on panel, signed with initials and dated *Sept 26 – 1861*
6½ × 20½ inches (16.5 × 52 cm)
PROVENANCE: The Duke of Hamilton, Hamilton Palace

## 72

HANS HANSEN RSW
1853–1947
*Waverley Station, Edinburgh,
1888*

Oil on canvas, signed lower right
6¾ × 9¾ inches (17.2 × 24.8 cm)

## 73

HANS HANSEN RSW
1853–1947
*Middle Eastern Interior*

Watercolour, signed lower right
9 × 11¼ inches
PROVENANCE: Rupert Christie

## 74

CHARLES HARRISON
TOWNSEND
1851–1928
*Japanese Ornaments*

Drawing in black ink, signed with
initials *C.H.T* inscribed *Japanese
Ornaments* and *Shewing Analysis
of Pattern*
8 × 5¼ inches (20.3 × 13.3 cm)

Japanese
Ornaments

Shewing Analysis
of Pattern

C. H. T

75

KEITH HENDERSON
1883–1982
*Madame X, c.1925*

Watercolour over pencil, signed with initials
lower right: a label verso in the artist's hand
reads *Study of Head and hands | Keith
Henderson | corner (?) Buckleigh, Glos.*
5 × 4¼ inches (12.7 × 10.7 cm)

*Illustrated actual size*

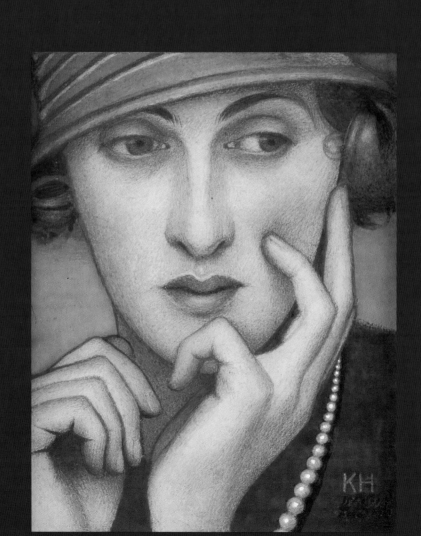

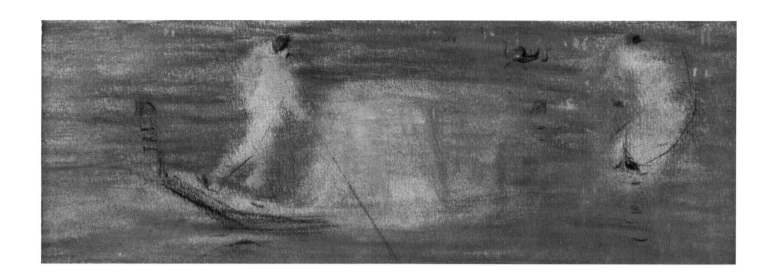

76

JAMES WATTERSTON HERALD
1859–1914
*Nocturne: Gondolas*

Pastel and charcoal on paper
3 × 8¼ inches (7.7 × 21 cm)

78

EDWARD ATKINSON HORNEL
1864–1933
*Pigs in the Wood*, 1887

Oil on canvas, signed and dated
16 × 12 inches (40.6 × 30.5 cm)
LITERATURE: Roger Billcliffe, *The Glasgow Boys*
London 1985 pp.193–4 no.185; Bill Smith, *Hornel:
The Life and Work of Edward Atkinson Hornel*,
Edinburgh 1997, p.45 (illustrated p.15).

## 77

**EDWARD ATKINSON HORNEL**
1864–1933
*Japanese Figures in a Garden*, 1896

Oil on canvas laid on board, signed and dated *E A Hornel 96*, lower left and inscribed *Tokio* · 14½ × 17½ inches (36.8 × 44.5 cm)

PROVENANCE: Liverpool Artists Club, a gift from the artist; sold in 1977
EXHIBITED: Edinburgh, The Fine Art Society, *Scottish Painting 1777–1927* 1977 (66) illustrated p.3; Glasgow, the Art Gallery, Edinburgh, Scottish Arts Council Gallery, Ayr, McLaurin Art Gallery, Inverness, Museum and Art Gallery, London, The Fine Art Society *Mr Henry & Mr Hornel visit Japan* (76), 1978 illustrated p.51; Tokyo, Mitsukoshi, *The Life & Times of Queen Victoria* 1979; Glasgow, Roger Billcliffe Gallery *E A Hornel 1868–1933* 1983 (6)
LITERATURE: Roger Billcliffe, *The Glasgow Boys* London, 1985 p.260 no.240

Early in 1893 Hornel and George Henry set off for Japan and they stayed for a year and a half. Inspired by Alfred East, they decided to go and see the country for themselves. They returned with a large body of work and the influence of Japan remained with Hornel throughout his life.

## 79

DENNIS HOUGHTON
*Self portrait, c.1940*
Oil on board
9 × 7 inches (22.8 × 17.8 cm)

## 80

SIR HARRY (HAMILTON) JOHNSTON GCMG KCB
1858–1927
*Part of the Garden of the British Consulate, La Marsa, Tunis, c.1897*

Oil on canvas, signed with monogram lower right
21 × 8 inches (5.5 × 20 cm)
Johnston served as HM Consul in Tunis from 1897–9.

## 81

WILLIAM KENNEDY RSA
1860–1918
*The Piper, 1885*

Oil on canvas, signed and dated
18 × 12 inches (46 × 30.5 cm)
LITERATURE: Roger Billcliffe, *The Glasgow Boys*, London, 1985,
no.190 illustrated p.199

## 82

WILLIAM KENNEDY RSA
1860–1918
*Stirling Station*, 1888

Oil on canvas, signed and inscribed *Stirling Station* lower left and
*William Kennedy* lower right
20½ × 31½ inches (52 × 80 cm)
PROVENANCE: Mrs Violet Mackay until 1970
EXHIBITED: Glasgow, Institute of Fine Arts, 1888, (203); New English
Art Club, 1890 (28); Munich, Glaspalast Exhibition, 1890; Stirling,
Fine Art Association, 1932; London, Royal Academy of Arts, 1939
(337); Glasgow, Scottish Arts Council, *The Glasgow Boys*, 1968 (69);
London, FAS, *The Glasgow School*, 1970 (20); Edinburgh, FAS, *100
Years of Scottish Painting*, 1973 (62); Stirling, MacRobert Centre, *The
Kailyard & The Glue Pot*, 1974–5 (26); Stirling, Smith Art Gallery,
Artists of Craigmill and Cambuskenneth, 1978 (20); RGIFA, 1978
(330); Glasgow & Edinburgh, FAS, *Glasgow 1900*, 1979 (34); London,
Hayward Gallery *Landscape in Britain 1850–1950* 1983 (90); London,
Christie's, NEAC Centenary Exhibition, 1986 (44); London, Barbican
Art Gallery *British Impressionism*, 1995 (106), illustrated p.49;
Glasgow, McLellan Galleries, *Scotland Creates*, 1990–1; Tokyo,
Diamura Museum; Tokushima Modern Art Museum; Osaka, Navio
Museum of Art, *British Impressionism*, 1997, no.34, illustrated p.65
LITERATURE: Roger Billcliffe, *The Glasgow Boys*, London, 1985,
pp200–1 no.182

Nowhere is William Kennedy's essential modernity more clearly
stated than in *Stirling Station*, 1888. An artist who until recently had
been painting peasants and whose consistent commitment to military
genre earned him the nickname, 'the Colonel', has temporarily
abandoned these pursuits for the spectacle of modern travel. A train is
expected, the trunks are ready for loading, the passengers have been
called and a Scottish station platform comes to life.

Kennedy is reputed to have worked privately with Bastien-Lepage
and Raphael Collin while he was a student in Paris in the ateliers of
Julian and Colarossi in the early 1880s. Following John Lavery, he
made his way to Grez-sur-Loing in 1884, where he painted *Spring*
(Renfrew Museums and Galleries) and *Mlle Cunegonde* (unlocated),
before returning to Scotland to establish a studio in Stirling. His
presence drew the other Glasgow Boys to the city and although he and
E.A.Walton proposed that they should form a society, of which
Kennedy should be President, this never materialised. Nevertheless in
the self-help group that emerged, he occupied a central role. Despite
this prominence, accurately dateable early pictures are comparatively
rare and of these *Stirling Station* occupies a special place.

Looking back to tearful farewells in London railway stations,
painted by Frank Holl, Hubert von Herkomer and James Tissot in the
1870s, Kennedy's canvas lacks their sentimentality. Whilst he might
have seen one of Monet's depictions of *Gare St Lazaire* during his

student years, he is more likely to have been attracted to Sydney
Starr's ambitious *Paddington Station* in 1886. However, had he seen
Starr's picture, the faults would have been obvious.

Although the passengers on Kennedy's platform are as persuasive
as those in Starr, there is no attempt to arrange them in anecdotal
groupings. His Highlander, seen in the detail he drew for *Quiz*, is
recognisable, but he is no more than a colourful figure in the waiting
crowd. In presenting the daily flow of travellers Kennedy was closest
in spirit to the Irish painter, Walter Osborne, whose *Hastings
Station*, c.1889 also addresses a provincial railway platform, brought
to life by the arrival of a steam train.

Kennedy's interest in contemporary reporting essentially goes
back to his Paris days. One extraordinary moment of these early
years, *Les Derniers Jours des Tuileries*, 1883, documents the
demolition of the ruins of a palace which had, for twelve years, stood
as a gaunt reminder of the dark days of the Commune. Kennedy
pictures the scene on a wet night, when the central city
thoroughfare, depicted by Manet in happier times, becomes a place of
desolation. Applying the medium to immediate circumstances –
those of a particular time of day – lay dormant until *Stirling Station*,
where the events are cast in the dying light of a late afternoon.

*Quiz*, in a lengthy review of the picture, noted that it stood out
'from all the crude, garish paint around it' and it was,

…one of the most remarkable pictures in the Exhibition,
displaying the consummate knowledge of the science of painting and
artistic technique possessed by the artist; the drawing, linear and
aerial perspective are most masterly; but it is in the exceptional skill
which the artist shows in his treatment of colour that the picture is
most remarkable. The unity of effect obtained through the delicate
harmonizing of each colour in relation to the general colour scheme,
the skilful management of the chiaroscuro and careful preservation
of values in the lighting of the work, make it exceedingly interesting
as an example of masterly, artistic craftsmanship, and well worth
careful study. The unusual truthfulness of the expression conveyed
by the picture gives it almost a prosaic and commonplace effect,
which is only saved by the admiration excited at the power and skill
of the artist.

At a time when reporters would often toss off a picture with glib
or sanctimonious comments, the paper penned a serious summation
of Kennedy's artistic achievement in *Stirling Station*, pointing to its
remarkable unity of effect in colour and tone, as well as its evident
'truthfulness'. The magazine concluded,

We hope to see him, ere long, manifesting his ability to conceive a
great and noble subject worthy of his exceptional power of artistic
expression, and carried out as successfully as this small work.

Kennedy may have thought to take up this challenge in *The
Deserter*, 1888. If so, it was a retrograde step – reverting to a subject
and treatment which recalls either Royal Academy social realist

'machines' by Hubert von Herkomer and Lady Butler. At the same
time, through its exhibition tour from Glasgow to London and on to
Munich, *Stirling Station* acquired an enviable array of plaudits, It is
undoubtedly true that the picture would have appealed to the
'London Impressionist' jurors of the New English Art Club for its
well-felt evening light. They too would have responded intuitively
to its self-evident modernity, and back in 1888, Lavery's crowd
scenes of the Glasgow International Exhibition would have been
lesser pictures without its example. The message was clear and
unequivocal and the picture's place in the history of Glasgow School
painting remains undiminished. Sadly, however, William Kennedy
never quite reclaimed the visionary intensity of that late afternoon
when a crowd assembles to catch a train at *Stirling Station*.
KENNETH MCCONKEY

83

JOHN KEPPIE RSA
1862–1945
*Broadway*, 1894

Watercolour on paper, signed and dated
*Sept 1894* lower right
11¾ × 11¾ inches (29.5 × 29.5 cm)

84

ETHEL KIRKPATRICK
*c.*1870–1941
*Edge of the Wood*, 1895

Oil on panel, signed and dated
13½ × 9½ inches (34.5 × 24 cm)

85

WINIFRED KNIGHTS
1899–1947
*Study for Paradise*, 1921

Watercolour and ink over pencil
8 × 10 inches (20 × 25.5 cm)

**86**

FRANK LAING
1862–1907
*Theatre du Sarah Bernhardt,
Paris, c.*1900

Watercolour over pencil, signed
*F Laing* lower left
14 × 12⅝ inches (35 × 31.5 cm)

**87**

FRANK LAING
1862–1907
*Place de la Concorde, c.*1900

Watercolour and pencil
5½ × 11 inches (14 × 28 cm)

**88**

FRANK LAING
1862–1907
*Nethergate, Dundee,* 1904

Monochrome wash
13 × 11½ inches (33 × 29cm)

**89**

FRANK LAING
1862–1907
*Looking West to Nethergate,
Dundee,* 1896

Watercolour, signed lower centre
21½ × 15 inches (52 × 38 cm)

**90**

FRANK LAING
1862–1907
*City Square*

Watercolour, signed lower centre
5½ × 11 inches (14 × 28 cm)

**91**

ROBERT SCOTT LAUDER RSA
1803–1869
*Study of a Huntsman*

Oil on board
8¼ × 6¾ inches (21 × 17cm)

## 92

SIR JOHN LAVERY RA RSA
1856–1941
*The Blue Hungarians*, 1888

Oil on canvas
12 × 14 inches (30.4 × 35.8 cm)
EXHIBITED: Glasgow, Craibe Angus Gallery 1888; Edinburgh, The Fine Art Society, *Scottish Painting 1777–1927*, 1977 (76); Edinburgh, London, Belfast and Dublin, The Fine Art Society, The Ulster Museum and the National Gallery of Ireland, *Sir John Lavery RA 1856–1941* 1984–5 (29); Glasgow, The Fine Art Society, *John Lavery and the Glasgow International Exhibition 1888* 1988; London, Barbican Art Gallery, *Impressionism in Britain* 1995 (118)
LITERATURE: The Scottish Art Review, vol.1, 1888, p.181 (illus); Roger Billcliffe, *The Glasgow Boys*, London, 1985, p.220 no.213; Stanley K Hunter, *Kelvingrove and the 1888 Exhibition of Industry, Science and Art, Glasgow, 1888*, 1990 (privately printed by the Exhibition Study Group), p.138; Kenneth McConkey, *Sir John Lavery*, Edinburgh 1993 p.56 (illustrated p.54)

In October 1888, Lavery staged an exhibition of fifty pieces executed during the Glasgow International Exhibition. This large display of the arts and manufactures of Great Britain and its trading partners across the world, was akin to the Great Exhibition at Crystal Palace. Officially opened on 8 May by its honorary president, Edward, Prince of Wales, it was housed in a temporary building designed by James Sellars, on the banks of the Kelvin, overlooked by the dour Gothic lecture halls of Glasgow University.

During the summer months Lavery produced over fifty small oils showing all aspects of the event. Interiors showing the sculpture gallery and the tea houses were juxtaposed with views of the Bishop's Palace and gondolas on the Kelvin. An impressive evening scene shows crowds approaching the domed entrance to the main building while selected performers such as Daniel Santiagoe, the famous curry cook, sat for head studies. He recorded performances like the musical ride of the 15th Hussars during the military tournament and the band of the Seaforth Highlanders, and when, on 22 August, Queen Victoria arrived for a state visit, the painter was on hand to record the event in a rapid oil sketch.

The Glasgow International turned Lavery into an 'artist-reporter'. Thereafter he could set up his easel in any circumstance and record the scene. He acquired the ability to compose spontaneously and to develop a personal shorthand which enabled the confusing detail of a moving crowd to be convincingly portrayed. All of these attributes are evident in the present canvas.

*The Blue Hungarians* shows William Johnson's Blue Gypsy String Band, conducted by Herr Barzea, playing at the North Kiosk, between 4 and 25 June.
KENNETH MCCONKEY

## 93

SIR JOHN LAVERY RA RSA
1856–1941
*A Grey Summer's Day, Grez,* 1883

Oil on canvas, signed and dated *J Lavery 1883*, lower left
7½ × 9½ inches (19 × 24.3 cm)
PROVENANCE: E A Walton; thence by descent until 1982
EXHIBITED: Glasgow & London, FAS, *Guthrie and the
Scottish Realists,* 1981 (65); St Andrews, Crawford Centre
for the Arts, *John Lavery, The Early Career,* 1983 (5);
Edinburgh, London, Belfast and Dublin, FAS, The Ulster
Museum and the National Gallery of Ireland, *Sir John
Lavery RA 1856–1941,* 1984–5, (7); Yamanashi
Prefectural Museum of Art, Fuchu Art Museum, Otani;
Memorial Museum of Art, Nariwa Museum & Sakura
City Museum of Art, Japan, *The Painters in Grez-sur-
Loing,* 2000–2001(15) illustrated p.65
LITERATURE: Kenneth McConkey, *From Grez to Glasgow,
French Naturalist Influence in Scottish Painting* The
Scottish Art Review, vol.xv, no.4, 1982, p.29 (illus p.30);
Roger Billcliffe, *The Glasgow Boys,* 1985, p.89 (illus p.83);
Kenneth McConkey, *Sir John Lavery,* Edinburgh 1993,
p.32 illustrated p.30

Despite its size, *A Grey Summer's Day, Grez* is a work of
enormous consequence in Lavery's *oeuvre.* Not only does
it reveal his seizure of the essential principles of French
naturalistic representation, but it also points to the future
in his artistic development. Its striking composition, close
observation of local colour, sensitivity to atmosphere and
the dramatic tension implied by the figures and dog, all
indicate an extraordinary precocity which sets Lavery
apart from the Galsgow painters to whom he would
return after his sojourns in the idyllic French village of
Grez-sur-Loing. *A Grey Summer's Day, Grez* is an early
masterpiece. KENNETH MCCONKEY

*Illustrated actual size*

94

SIR JOHN LAVERY RA RSA
1856–1941
*Woman in Profile*, 1883

Oil on canvas, signed and dated *J Lavery 1883* upper right
18 × 18 inches (45.5 × 45.5 cm)
EXHIBITED: Edinburgh, FAS, *Scottish Painting 1800–1950*, 1975,
no.53; Glasgow and Edinburgh, FAS, *Glasgow 1900*, 1979, no.43 (illus
in cat.); Glasgow and London, FAS, *Guthrie and the Scottish Realists*,
1981 (63); Edinburgh, London, Belfast and Dublin, FAS, The Ulster
Museum and the National Gallery of Ireland, *Sir John Lavery RA*,
1984–5, no.5
LITERATURE: Roger Billcliffe, *The Glasgow Boys*, 1985, p.81 (illus
p.80); Kenneth McConkey, *Sir John Lavery*, 1993, p.24 (illus p.25)

Mystery surrounds the identity of Lavery's early models. His
Glasgow pictures in the mid-1880s for instance, often contain a
young, red-haired woman who remains unnamed. While in Paris
and Grez-sur-Loing between November 1881 and December 1884, a
number of other models – art student contemporaries, hotel-maids
and villagers – appear in his work. In some cases the same face or the
same dress is carried from picture to picture, creating sub-sets within
the overall pattern of production. Two works which have been linked
because they seem to relate to one another are *A Quiet Day in the
Studio*, 1883 and *Woman in Profile*, 1883, the present picture. Both
seem to represent the same woman and both are exceptionally fine
studies of tone, revealing a similar lightness of touch.

In its own terms, *Woman in Profile* demonstrates the artist's
thorough understanding of current atelier practice. The handling –
using square brushstrokes – shows Lavery's personal approach to
methods commonly found in the work of his British expatriate
contemporaries. The *contre jour* effect complicates the exercise. For
the first time however, no attempt is made to suggest that this is
anything other than a contemporary woman. She is not a 'Gretchen'
or a 'Marguerite'. There are no costumes or theatre props. Installed
in Paris, Lavery moved away from such devices, and what we see
here is a simple, direct confrontation with a young woman – with
obvious *hauteur*. KENNETH MCCONKEY

## 95

EDWARD LEAR
1812–1888
*Sheik Saleh*, 1849

Ink and wash over pencil on paper, inscribed *Sheikh Saleh 5. Feb. 3.p.m. 1849 (near Suez)*, lower left, and *pipe should be straight* and numbered *202*, lower right · 11 × 8¾ inches (28 × 22.3 cm)
PROVENANCE: Dr Giorgio Ajmone Marsan

## 96

EDWARD LEAR
1812–1888
*String of Camels*, 1849

Ink over pencil on paper, inscribed in ink and in pencil *Feb 6, 1849, 7am*, lower left, and numbered *206*, lower right · 2⅝ × 10 inches (7 × 25.5cm)
PROVENANCE: Dr Giorgio Ajmone Marsan

## 97

EDWARD LEAR
1812–1888
*Arabs and Camels*, 1849

Ink over pencil on paper, inscribed in ink *February 5 1849 3–4 p.m. near Suez* and numbered *204*, lower right, with other annotations
4 × 9½ inches (10 × 24 cm)
PROVENANCE: Dr Giorgio Ajmone Marsan

## 98

FREDERIC, LORD LEIGHTON OF STRETTON PRA
1830–1896
*Athlete Wrestling with a Python*, c.1874

Bronze
9½ inches (24.5cm) high (stand is 52 inches)
PROVENANCE: Charles and Lavinia Handley-Read
EXHIBITED: London, Royal Academy of Arts, *Victorian and Edwardian Decorative Art: The Handley-Read Collection* 1972 (F37–39)

Leighton conceived this, his first known sculpture, when modelling some of the figures for *The Daphnephoria* in the early 1870s, a life-size model was exhibited at the Royal Academy in 1877. Few of this smallest size are recorded: one in bronze appears in a number of Leighton's paintings of the interior of his studio. This sculpture is an icon of what is now described as 'The New Sculpture'.

99

ARTHUR LEMON
1850–1912
*On the Viale, Florence, c.1885*
Oil on panel · 7½ × 12 inches (19 × 30.5cm)

100

HELEN LESSORE
1907–1994
*Berkeley Square, London*
Oil on canvas · 25 × 30 inches (63.5 × 76 cm)

101

LADY ELIZABETH LYTTELTON
DIED 1795
AFTER JEAN-ETIENNE LIOTARD 1707–89
*Portrait of Mary Gunning, Countess of Coventry*

Watercolour over pencil on vellum, signed and
dated *E Lyttelton* | *1755* · 9 × 7 inches (23 × 18cm)

## 102

JAMES PITTENDRIGH MACGILLIVRAY RSA
1856–1938

*An East Coast Close*, 1882

Oil on canvas, signed and dated *J.P.McGillivray* 1882,
lower left
16⅜ × 10⅝ inches (41.5 × 27 cm)
EXHIBITED: Aberdeen Art Gallery, *James Pittendrigh
Macgillivray 1856–1938*, 1988

## 103

JAMES PITTENDRIGH MACGILLIVRAY RSA
1856–1938

*Sir George Reid* PRSA

Bronze, signed *J.P. McGillivray*, rear of left shoulder,
inscribed with anthemion and numbered '6' on
granite base
10 inches (25.3 cm) high

## 104

CHARLES HODGE MACKIE RSA RSW
1862–1920

*Hillside with Sheep*

Oil on board
9 × 6½ inches (23 × 16.5cm)

## 105

ROBERT MCGREGOR RSA
1848–1922

*Culross, Fife, c.*1900

Oil on board, signed with initials
8½ × 5 inches (21.5 × 13cm)

## 106

PAUL MAITLAND
1863–1909
*Chimneys at Battersea*, 1908

Oil on panel
3⅞ × 6½ inches (9.5 × 16.5cm)

## 107

PAUL MAITLAND
1863–1909
*Plumbago Works, Battersea,*
*1907*

Oil on panel, signed with initials PM,
lower right
4⅝ × 6½ inches (11.7 × 16.5 cm)

## 108

PAUL MAITLAND
1863–1909
*Edith Terrace, Chelsea*

Oil on panel, signed *Maitland*, lower
right
9½ × 5¾ inches (24.2 × 14.8 cm)
EXHIBITED: London, The Fine Art
Society, *Paul Fordyce Maitland*, 1994
(14)

## 109

PAUL MAITLAND
1863–1909
*Kensington Gardens*

Oil on canvas, signed *P Maitland*, lower left
12⅛ × 16¼ inches (30.7 × 41.3 cm)
EXHIBITED: London, The Fine Art Society, *Paul Fordyce Maitland*, 1994 (33)

## 110

PAUL MAITLAND
1863–1909
*Rochester seen from the Medway*

Oil on canvas, signed *P Maitland*, lower left
24 × 29 inches (61 × 73.7 cm)
PROVENANCE: Anthony Carroll
EXHIBITED: London, The Leicester Galleries, *Paul Maitland*, 1962 (52); London, The Fine Art Society, *Paul Fordyce Maitland*, 1994 (35)

## 111

PAUL MAITLAND
1863–1909
*Battersea, 1906*

Oil on canvas, signed *Paul Maitland*, lower left
13 × 17 inches (33 × 43cm)

### 112

ALEXANDER MANN
1853–1908
*The Souk, Tangier*

Oil on board · 5½ × 9 inches (14 × 23cm)
PROVENANCE: Estate of the Artist

### 113

LOUIS MARCOUSSIS
1883–1941
*Serge Lifar*, 1933

Etching and engraving, signed in pencil *L Marcoussis*, lower right:
numbered 31 from the edition of 50 , 16¾ × 9½ inches (42.5 × 23.8 cm)
PROVENANCE: Sir Rex Nan Kivell

### 114

JAMES McBEY
1883–1959
*Marrakesh*, 1938

Etching, signed in ink *James McBey*, lower right, printed in black ink
on wove paper: from the edition of 60 · 11 × 9 inches (27.8 × 23.1 cm)
REFERENCE: Martin Hardie 274

## 115

ARTHUR MELVILLE ARSA RSW
1855–1904
*Les Laveuses*, 1880

Oil on panel, signed and dated *Arthur Melville 1890*, lower right
4½ × 17½ inches (11.5 × 44.5cm)
PROVENANCE: Marion Melville; Charles and Lavinia Handley-Read
EXHIBITED: Edinburgh, Royal Scottish Academy 1881 (233);
Glasgow, Glasgow Institute of Fine Arts, 1907 (103); London, The
Fine Art Society, *Centenary Exhibition* 1976 (112); Memorial
Museum of Art, Nariwa Museum and Sakura City Museum of Art,
Japan, *The Painters in Grez-sur-Loing*, 2000–2001 (14)
Literature: Agnes Mackay, *Arthur Meville*, London 1951, (176)
p.163; Iain Gale, *Arthur Melville*, Edinburgh 1996, p.20, pl.10

*Illustrated actual size*

116

ARTHUR MELVILLE ARSA RSW
1855–1904
*Two Girls in a Boat*, 1890

Pastel on paper · 29 × 12½ inches (74 × 32 cm)
LITERATURE: Agnes Mackay *Arthur Melville*, London,
p.151 (432); Iain Gale, *Arthur Melville*, Edinburgh 1996
pp63–64, pl.51
EXHIBITED: Edinburgh, Bourne Fine Art, London,
The Fine Art Society *Arthur Melville* 1996

117

ARTHUR MELVILLE ARSA RSW
1855–1904
*Scottish Farm by an Estuary*

Watercolour · 23 × 31 inches (58.5 × 79cm)

118

ARTHUR MELVILLE ARSA RSW
1855–1904
*Daisies*

Oil on canvas
8½ × 8½ inches (21.5 × 21.5cm)

## 119

ARTHUR MELVILLE ARSA RSW
1855–1904
*Water Lilies, c.*1890

Watercolour over pencil
11 × 17½ inches (28 × 44.5cm)
LITERATURE: Agnes Mackay, *Arthur Melville*, 1951, p, 151, (436)

120

ARTHUR MELVILLE ARSA RSW
1855–1904
*Cat and Kittens c.1890*

Watercolour and chinese white on buff paper
12 × 16 inches (30.5 × 40.5cm)
LITERATURE: Agnes Mackay, *Arthur Melville*, 1951, p.148 (363)

121

ARTHUR MELVILLE ARSA RSW
1855–1904
*The Bazaar at Vringa*

Watercolour
11 × 17½ inches (28 × 44.5cm)

122
ARTHUR MELVILLE
ARSA RSW
1855–1904
*A Cabbage Garden,
1877*

Oil on canvas, signed and dated *A. Melville 1877*, lower right
18 × 12 inches (46 × 30.5cm)
EXHIBITED: London, Royal Academy of Arts, 1878 (104); Edinburgh, Royal Scottish Academy, 1878 (687); Dundee, Museums and Art Galleries *Arthur Melville*, 1977 (3); London, Tate Britain, *Art of the Garden*, 2004 (5)
LITERATURE: Roger Billcliffe, *The Glasgow Boys*, London, 1985, p.26, 111 (102); Iain Gale, *Arthur Melville*, Edinburgh 1996, pl.1

## 123

MORTIMER MENPES
1855–1939
*Buildings by a River, Japan*

Watercolour, signed *Mortimer Menpes*, lower left
7¾ × 6½ inches (19.7 × 16.5cm)
EXHIBITED: London, The Fine Art Society,
*Opening the Window*, 1991 (42)

## 124

MORTIMER MENPES
1855–1939
*Japanese Woman with Flags*

Oil on panel, signed lower right
6 × 4⅜ inches (15 × 11cm)
EXHIBITED: London, Barbican Art Gallery,
*Impressionism in Britain* (137); London,
Barbican Art Gallery, *Wilde Years* 2000 (101);
London, The Fine Art Society, *Opening the
Window*, 1991 (35)

## 125

BERNARD BOUTET DE MONVEL
1881–1949
*Man on Camel in Battle*

Watercolour
8¾ × 14½ inches (22 × 37cm)
PROVENANCE: Chloe Blackburn

## 126

SIR WILLIAM QUILLER
ORCHARDSON RA
1832–1910
*Meditation, c.1860*

Oil on panel
6 × 4¾ inches (15.2 × 12.2 cm)

*Illustrated actual size*

126

127

SIR WILLIAM QUILLER
ORCHARDSON RA
1832–1910
*Solitude*

Oil on canvas
21½ × 27½ inches (54.5 × 69.8 cm)
EXHIBITED: Edinburgh, National
Gallery of Scotland, Aberdeen Art
Gallery *Master Class: Robert Scott
Lauder and his Pupils* 1983 (120)

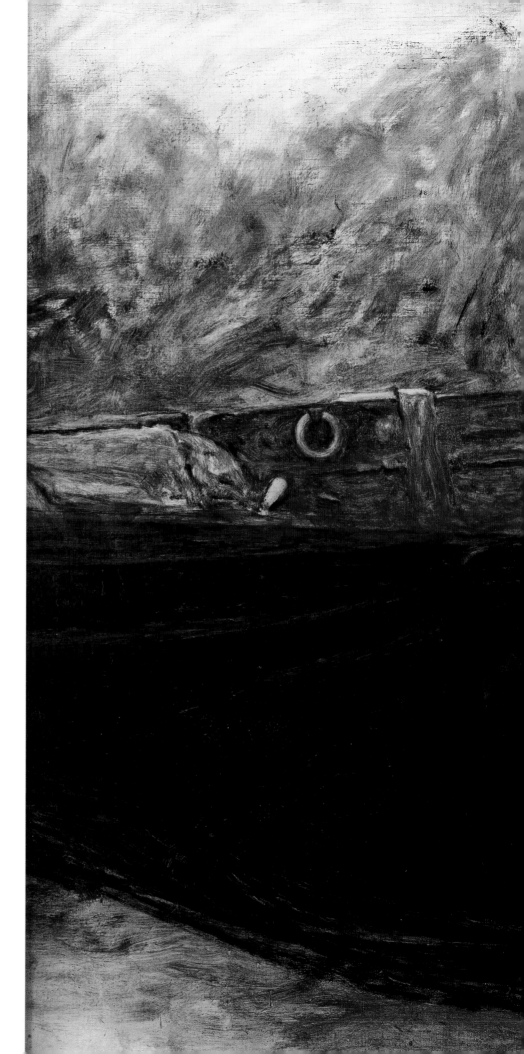

## 128

ALFRED BERTRAM PEGRAM
1873–1941
*Head of a Youth*

Metal, on marble base of square section, signed *A Bertram Pegram*,
on back of neck
9 inches (22.8 cm) including base: head 4½ inches (11.4 cm)

## 129

DAVID PIDDOCK
BORN 1960
*Self Portrait*

Oil on board · 6½ × 4¾ inches (16.5 × 11.5cm)

## 130

JOHN QUINTON PRINGLE
1864–1925
*The Family Promenade*

Pen and brown ink on paper
2 × 2¾ inches (5 × 7 cm)
PROVENANCE: Una Rota

## 131

ARTHUR PUTNAM
1873–1930
*Panther,* 1908

Bronze, inscribed *A PUTNAM | 08*
2½ × 10 × 4 inches (6.3 × 25.3 × 10 cm)

## 132

AGNES MIDDLETON RAEBURN RSW
1872–1955
*St. Varley Sur-Somme, Evening*

Oil on board, signed lower right
7 × 5 inches (18 × 13cm)
PROVENANCE: Una Rota

## 133

SIR GEORGE REID PRSA
1841–1913
*Duke Street, Edinburgh, under Snow, 1870*

Oil on canvas
9¾ × 6¾ inches (24.5 × 17cm)

## 134

SIR GEORGE REID PRSA
1841–1913
AFTER GEORGE JAMESONE 1589/90–1644
*Artist with Etchings*

Pen and ink, signed with monogram, upper right
5 × 6¼ inches (13 × 16cm)

## 135

GEORGE RICHMOND RA
1809–1896
*Study of Soldiers, 1838*

Gouache on card, signed dated and inscribed *Rome. 1838 G. Richmond*, lower left
9½ × 6¼ inches (24 × 16cm)

**136**

DAVID ROBERTS RA
1796–1864
*A Study of a Black Slave, Tangiers, 1833*

Watercolour over pencil on paper, inscribed *Tangiers March 30 1833*
*Study of a Black Slave* · 11½ × 8⅝ inches (29.2 × 22 cm)

## 137

FREDERICK CAYLEY ROBINSON
1862–1927
*Memories, A Study*

Oil on panel
6½ × 8 inches (16.5 × 20.5cm)
EXHIBITED: London, Leicester Galleries, 1929 (23)

## 138

THEODORE ROUSSEL
1847–1926
*The Little Gate, Chelsea (1889–1890)*

Etching and drypoint, signed in pencil *Theodore Roussel*, printed in black ink on paper trimmed to the platemark by the artist, leaving a signature tab: an impression in the fourth (final) state, one of about 43 in all
8⅛ × 6½ inches (20.8 × 16.5 cm)
PROVENANCE: A gift from Agnes Mackay (the artist's niece) and Marion Melville (the artist's stepdaughter), Paris 1968
REFERENCE: Hausberg 33 iv | IV

## 139

THEODORE ROUSSEL
1847–1926
*The Old Plumbago Works, Battersea, from Cheyne Walk, c.1890*

Oil on canvas
18 × 14 inches (46 × 35.5 cm)

140

MABEL ROYDS
1874–1941
*Concert: Eugene Ysaye (Violin) and
Raoul Pugno (Piano), c.1905*

Oil on canvas
11½ × 9¾ inches (29 × 24.5cm)

141

TOM SCOTT RSA RSW
1854–1927
*Contemplation, 1883*

Watercolour and gouache, signed and dated
*Tom Scott 83*, lower left
13½ × 6½ inches (34.5 × 16.5cm)

142

TOM SCOTT RSA RSW
1854–1927
*Artist painting by a Burn, 1886*

Watercolour heightened with Chinese white,
signed and dated *Tom Scott 86*, lower right
7¾ × 11½ inches (19.5 × 29cm)

## 143

THOMAS SEDDON
1821–1856

*Lieutenant Richard Burton in Arab Dress,* 1854

Watercolour on paper, signed, dated *T. Seddon 1854* and inscribed
*Egypt* lower right
11 × 7½ inches (28 × 19cm)
PROVENANCE: Sir Richard Burton; Lady Maria Sistel; Lillian Swain
(Mrs Black)
EXHIBITED: London, The Fine Art Society, *North African Traveller*
1974 (88) (illustrated front cover); Edinburgh, Scottish National
Portrait Gallery *Visions of the Ottoman Empire* 1994
LITERATURE: J.P.Seddon, *Memoirs and Letters of the late Thomas
Seddon, Artist* London, 1858 pp.32–33; Raymond Watkinson,
*Pre-Raphaelite Art and Design* London 1970, p.139; Allen Staley,
*The Pre-Raphaelite Landscape* Oxford 1973 p.98, note.

Seddon met Sir Richard Burton KCMG in 1853. This picture was
painted in Cairo for an account Seddon was going to publish of his
travels in Arabia, and his journey to Mecca.

*Illustrated actual size*

144

THOMAS SEDDON
1821–1856

*Arab and Dromedary: The Tomb of Babar-el-Sheik in the distance, Cairo*

Oil on canvas, signed *T Seddon* and inscribed *Egypt 1854*, lower right
10½ × 14 inches (27 × 35.5cm)
EXHIBITED: Edinburgh, Scottish National Portrait Gallery *Visions of the Ottoman Empire* 1994

## 145

WALTER SICKERT ARA
1860–1942
*The Bugler*

Watercolour over pencil, signed *Walter Sickert*, lower right,
and inscribed *On Loch Awe*, lower left
3¾ × 2⅜ inches (9.5 × 6.1 cm)
EXHIBITED: London, The Fine Art Society, 1888

## 146

JOSEPH EDWARD SOUTHALL
1861–1944
*Arnold Dolmetsch*, 1916

Watercolour over pencil, signed with monogram and dated
*8.v | 1916*, lower left, inscribed ARNOLD DOLMETSCH, upper left
4⅜ × 3 inches (11 × 7.7 cm)
PROVENANCE: Maxwell Ashby Armfield

## 147

JOSEPH EDWARD SOUTHALL
1861–1944
*Study of Fruit for 'New Lamps for Old'*, 1900

Watercolour, signed with monogram and dated *X. 1900*, lower left
5 × 4¼ inches (13 × 11cm)
PROVENANCE: Maxwell Ashby Armfield

## 148

ROBERT MACAULAY STEVENSON RSA
1854–1952
*Village on a Hill – The Silver Birch*

Oil on board, signed *Macaulay Stevenson*, lower left
11 × 6 inches (28 × 15cm)

## 149

ROBERT MACAULAY STEVENSON RSA
1854–1952
*Woodland by Moonlight*

Oil on canvas
20¼ × 24 inches (52 × 61cm)

## 150

WILLIAM STRANG RA RSA
1859–1921
*Portrait of a Man in a Grey Suit,* 1890

Oil on canvas, signed and dated *W Strang 90*, upper left
20 × 25 inches (51 × 63.5cm)
EXHIBITED: Sheffield, Graves Art Gallery, Glasgow,
Museums and Art Gallery, London, National Portrait
Gallery, *William Strang* RA, *Painter-Etcher*; 1991;
London, The Royal Society of Portrait Painters,
*Centenary Exhibition*, 1991 (24),

## 151

STANSMORE RICHMOND DEAN
(MRS ROBERT MACAULAY STEVENSON) 1866–1944
*Portrait of Robert Macaulay Stevenson*

Oil on canvas laid on board, signed *Stansmore
Stevenson*, lower left
6 × 4¼ inches (15 × 11cm)
PROVENANCE: Una K. Rota; a gift to Andrew McIntosh
Patrick, 1993
EXHIBITED: Kirkcudbright *Jubilee Exhibition*, 1982;
Glasgow Society of Women Artists, Lillie Gallery,
Milngavie, 1984 (13)

## 152

GRAHAM SUTHERLAND
1903–1980
*Textile Design*

Gouache
12 × 10 inches (30.5 × 25.3 cm)
PROVENANCE: Gift from Elsbeth Juda
EXHIBITED: Sheffield, Graves Art Gallery, *Juda
Collection*, 1967 (121)

## 153

SIR WILLIAM HAMO THORNYCROFT
1850–1925
*Charles George Gordon*, 1888

Bronze, marked on the base, HAMO THORNYCROFT | SC
1888
14½ inches (36.8 cm) high

## 154

DAVID TINDLE RA
BORN 1932
*The Harvest*

Oil on board
6 × 8¼ inches (15.2 × 21 cm)

## 155

FÉLIX VALLOTTON
1865–1925
*L'Enfant au beret*, 1889

Etching, stamped with the monogram *FV*, lower left,
printed in black ink on wove paper: numbered 24 from
the edition of 30, with the blindstamp 'Atelier F.
Vallotton'
10⅛ × 9 inches (25.8 × 22.7 cm)

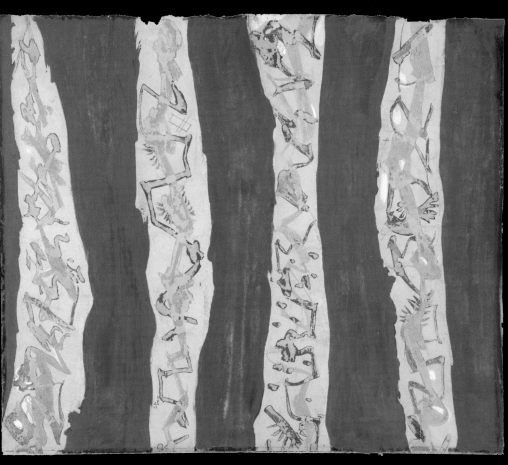

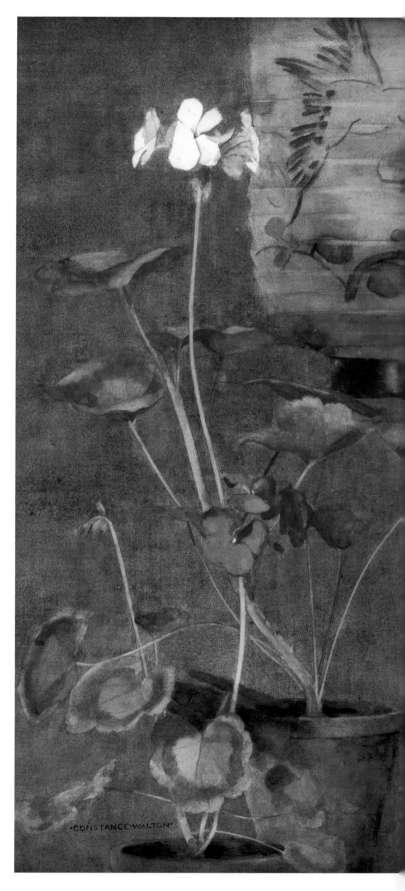

## 156

JAN CORNELIUS VAN ESSEN
1854–1936
*A Marabou Stork*, 1899

Oil on panel, signed and dated *Jan van Essen 1899*,
lower right, and inscribed *Maraboe*, upper left
11 × 7½ inches (28 × 19 cm)

## 157

CONSTANCE WALTON RSW
1865–1960
*Geraniums and a Japanese Lantern*

Watercolour, signed *Constance Walton*, lower left
21 × 9½ inches (53.5 × 24cm)

**158**

EDWARD ARTHUR WALTON RSA PRSW
1860–1922

*By the Stream, Autumn*, 1882

Oil on canvas, signed and dated *E A Walton 82*, lower left and
inscribed verso 'By the Stream'
11 × 24 inches (28 × 61 cm)

## 159

EDWARD ARTHUR WALTON RSA PRSW
1860–1922
*A Herd Boy,* 1886

Watercolour, signed and dated *E.A.Walton '86,* lower right
21 × 22½ inches (53.5 × 57cm)
EXHIBITED: Edinburgh, The Royal Scottish Society of Painters in
Watercolour, 1886 (1106)
LITERATURE: Roger Billcliffe, *The Glasgow Boys,* London 1985 p.132
(illustrated); Fiona MacSporran, *Edward Arthur Walton 1860–1922,*
Glasgow 1987 pp.31–2

*A Herd Boy* confirms that Walton's figures no longer play a
secondary role in his overall compositions. Attention is focused on
the boy who is centrally placed among the colourful grasses of the
hillside. The whole picture is dominated by the gloriously powerful
blue of the boy's jacket. The continued influence of Bastien-Lepage
is revealed in the peasant clothing, weathered hat and heavily shod
feet, although the fresh cloudy sky and browsing cows are both
characteristic of nobody but Walton himself.

**160**

ELIJAH WALTON
1833–1880
*Homeward Bound in Sinai,*
1876

Watercolour and pencil on paper,
signed and dated *Elijah Walton 1876,*
lower right
6¾ × 4⅜ inches (17 × 11cm)

**161**

JOHN DAWSON WATSON
1832–1892
*Portrait of a Gentleman,* 1880

Oil on panel, signed *J Watson,* lower
left
7½ × 10½ inches (19 × 26.5cm)

**162**

PHILIP WEBB
1831–1915
*The Lion Astir,* 1867

Ink on tinted paper, signed with
monogram *PW,* lower left, heightened
with white, inscribed in another hand,
verso 'Drawn by Philip Webb in 1867'
5¼ × 6¾ inches (13.3 × 17.2 cm)
EXHIBITED: London, The Fine Art
Society, *William Morris and
Company,* 1979 (221)

## 163

JAMES MᴄNEILL WHISTLER
1834–1903

*Chelsea Arts Club (A house with a veranda and steps leading to a garden)*

Dark brown ink on paper, signed with a butterfly, centre right
2¾ × 4½ inches (6.8 × 11.6 cm)
PROVENANCE: Theodore Roussel, a gift from the artist; Ethel Melville, Roussel's second wife; Marion Melville
LITERATURE: Margaret F MacDonald, *James McNeill Whistler: Drawings, Pastels, and Watercolours: A Catalogue Raisonné*, New Haven and London 1995 p.435 no.1194

## 164

JAMES MᴄNEILL WHISTLER
1834–1903

*Chelsea Arts Club (A door opening onto steps down to a garden)*

Dark brown ink on paper, signed with a butterfly, centre right
2¾ × 4¾ inches (7 × 12 cm)
PROVENANCE: Theodore Roussel, a gift from the artist; Ethel Melville, Roussel's second wife; Marion Melville
LITERATURE: Margaret F MacDonald, *James McNeill Whistler: Drawings, Pastels, and Watercolours: A Catalogue Raisonné*, New Haven and London 1995 pp.434–35 no.1193

## 165

WILLIAM HEATH WILSON
1849–1927
*Venetian Scene*, 1888

Oil on panel, inscribed *Venice*
4½ × 2¾ inches (11.5 × 7cm)

## 166

WILLIAM HEATH WILSON
1849–1927
*Bridge at Chioggia*, 1888

Oil on panel, inscribed *Bridge at Chioggia*
4½ × 2¾ inches (11.5 × 6.5cm)

## 167

WILLIAM HEATH WILSON
1849–1927
*A Boat at Luxor Moored at Night*, c.1890

Oil on board, signed *W H Wilson*, lower left
4⅞ × 7⅞ inches (12.4 × 19.8 cm)

## 168

ANTON VAN WOUW
1862–1945
*A Shangaan*, 1907

Bronze, signed, inscribed and dated on torso,
*A van Wouw S.A. Joh-burg | 1907*, base
inscribed: *G. Massa | Fuse-*ROMA
12 inches (30.5 cm) high

A cast of this sculpture was exhibited
at The Fine Art Society in *Anton van
Wouw Bronze Statuettes*, 1909 (1)
priced at £12.12.0

*Part Two · Furniture & the Decorative Arts*

265

## 169

AESTHETIC MOVEMENT
*Music cabinet, c.1875*

Rosewood with engraved bronze hinges, escutcheon and castors, the central door panel with Japanese gilded lacquer decoration
47⅞ × 19⅝ × 13¾ inches (121.7 × 49.8 × 34.9 cm)
EXHIBITED: London, Barbican Art Gallery; Tokyo, Setagaya Art Museum, *Japan and Britain: An Aesthetic Dialogue 1850–1930*, 1991–2 (116)
LITERATURE: Tomoko Sato and Toshio Watanabe, editors, *Japan and Britain: An Aesthetic Dialogue 1850–1930*, exhibition catalogue, 1991 (Barbican Art Gallery) p.114 (illus.) p.117

## 170

AESTHETIC MOVEMENT
*Hanging cabinet, c.1875*

Stained wood, tooled and gilded leather, and Japanese textile
30¾ × 17¼ × 8 inches (78.1 × 43.8 × 20.3 cm)
Showing the influence of the designers E.W. Godwin and H.W. Batley

## 171

AESTHETIC MOVEMENT
*Tub-back chair, c.1875*

Ebonized wood with replacement upholstery
26½ × 25½ × 25 inches (63 × 64.8 × 63.5 cm)
This chair was designed in the manner of E. W. Godwin; see, for instance, *Art Furniture Designed by Edward W. Godwin FSA and Manufactured by William Watt* (London, 1877), pl.14

## 172

AESTHETIC MOVEMENT
*Centre table, c.1880*

Turned, carved and ebonized wood with gilded decoration
28 inches (71.1 cm) high, 37½ inches (95.3 cm) dia.

## 173

AESTHETIC MOVEMENT
POSSIBLY FRENCH
*Cloisonné box, c.1880*

1⅞ inches (4.7 cm) high, 4⅜ inches (11.1 cm) dia.

## 174

AESTHETIC MOVEMENT
*Pair of firedogs, designed before 1885*

Cast iron, each foot with an indistinct cast registration mark
6¼ × 7 × 4 inches (15.9 × 17.8 × 10.2 cm)

## 175

AESTHETIC MOVEMENT
*Trivet, the design registered 1882*

Brass, with registration mark for 18 January 1882
⅝ × 7⅜ × 7⅜ inches (1.6 × 18.7 × 18.7 cm)

## 176

THOMAS ALLEN 1831–1915 [DESIGNER]
WEDGWOOD, ETRURIA, AND J. HINKS AND SON LTD, BIRMINGHAM [MANUFACTURERS]
*'Playmates' lamp, c.1875*

Hand-painted and gilded transfer-ware ceramic, later cut-glass font mounted with original fittings for oil variously stamped HINKS'S | DUPLEX | PATENT, the whole on a bronze base, the underside impressed J. HINKS & SON LIMITED | 2244
15¾ inches (40 cm) high excluding chimney
EXHIBITED: London, Camden Arts Centre, *The Aesthetic Movement, 1869–1890*, 1973 (106)
LITERATURE: Charles Spencer, editor, *The Aesthetic Movement, 1869–1890*, exhibition catalogue (London, 1973), illus. facing p.49 and p.72 cat.106

314    176    313

288

## 177

ALLANDER POTTERY, MILNGAVIE

*Covered Jar,* 1906

Base incised *Allander* | *364* | *1906* | painted monogram
4 inches (10.2 cm)

## 178

ADRIAN ALLINSON 1890–1959

*Virgin and Child, c.*1930

Glazed terracotta, incised ALLINSON, verso
22¾ inches (57.8 cm)
PROVENANCE: James McIntosh Patrick OBE RSA (1907–98)

## 179

ARTS AND CRAFTS

*Pair of tripod stands*

Stained oak
12⅛ × 18¾ inches (30.7 × 47.6 cm) dia.

## 180

ARTS AND CRAFTS

*Ceramic plaque with symbols of the Union, c.*1890

16¼ × 16¼ inches (41.3 × 41.3 cm)

## 181

ART MOVEMENT

*Ottoman, c.*1870

Ebonized, painted and gilded wood, the hinged top with replacement
horsehair upholstery
19½ × 15 × 35 inches (49.5 × 38 × 89 cm)

This ottoman is designed in a style strongly reminiscent of the work
of Richard Norman Shaw or William Eden Nesfield

181

## 182

ART MOVEMENT

*Drop-leaf table, c.*1870

Mahogany with incised and ebonized moulding
28¾ × 31¼ × 16 inches (73 × 79.4 × 40.6 cm), the top 23⅜inches
(59.4 cm) square when raised

This table has design characteristics associated with Charles Bevan
and Charles Locke Eastlake

## 183

WILLIAM AULT
SWADLINCOTE [MANUFACTURER]

*Vase,* the design registered 1892

Underside impressed with manufacturer's cipher | RD 195324
2½ inches (6.4 cm)

## 184

WILLIAM AULT
SWADLINCOTE [MANUFACTURER]

*Vase,* the design registered 1892

Underside impressed with manufacturer's cipher | RD 195324
3¼ inches (8.3 cm)

## 185

WILLIAM AULT
SWADLINCOTE [MANUFACTURER]

*Vase,* the design registered 1892

Underside impressed with manufacturer's cipher | RD 195324
3¼ inches (8.3 cm)

## 186

WILLIAM AULT
SWADLINCOTE [MANUFACTURER]

*Vase,* the design registered 1892

Underside impressed with manufacturer's cipher | RD 195324
3¼ inches (8.3 cm)

## 187

WILLIAM AULT
SWADLINCOTE [MANUFACTURER]

*Vase,* the design registered 1892

Underside impressed with manufacturer's cipher | RD 195324
2½ inches (6.4 cm)

## 188

WILLIAM AULT
SWADLINCOTE [MANUFACTURER]

*Vase,* the design registered 1892

Underside impressed with manufacturer's cipher | RD 195324
4½ inches (11.4 cm)

183–190 & 310

## 189

**WILLIAM AULT**
SWADLINCOTE [MANUFACTURER]

*Vase*, the design registered 1892

Underside impressed with manufacturer's cipher | RD 195324
4½ inches (11.4 cm)

## 190

**WILLIAM AULT**
SWADLINCOTE [MANUFACTURER]

*Vase*, the design registered 1892

Underside impressed with manufacturer's cipher | RD 195324 |
ENGLAND | 215 | H
8⅛ inches (20.6 cm)

## 191

**WILLIAM AULT**
SWADLINCOTE [MANUFACTURER]

*Ornament, c.1887*

7¼ inches (18.4 cm) dia.

## 192

**WILLIAM AULT**
SWADLINCOTE [ATTRIBUTED MANUFACTURER]

*Cluster vase, c.1887*

6½ inches (16.5 cm)

## 193

**WILLIAM AULT**
SWADLINCOTE [ATTRIBUTED MANUFACTURER]

*Vase, c.1887*

5⅞ inches (14.9 cm)

**194**

WILLIAM AULT
SWADLINCOTE [ATTRIBUTED MANUFACTURER]
*Cluster vase, c.1887*

6 inches (15.2 cm)

**195**

WILLIAM AULT
SWADLINCOTE [ATTRIBUTED MANUFACTURER]
*Hanging vase c.1887*

9⅛ inches (23.2 cm) dia.

**196**

GILBERT BAYES PRBS
1872–1953 [DESIGNER] DOULTON [MANUFACTURER]
*Thistle finial, 1931–8*

13¼ inches (33.7 cm) high 14¾ inches (37.5 cm) high including ebonized wood base

PROVENANCE: Commissioned for the York Rise estate by the St Pancras Housing Association, London

LITERATURE: Paul Atterbury and Louise Irvine, *Gilbert Bayes Sculptor 1872–1953* (Richard Dennis, 1998), p.172

**197**

GILBERT BAYES PRBS
1872–1953 [DESIGNER] DOULTON [MANUFACTURER]
*Rose finial, 1931–8*

13⅝ inches (34.6 cm) high 15 inches (38.1 cm) high including ebonized wood base

PROVENANCE: Commissioned for the York Rise estate by the St Pancras Housing Association, London

LITERATURE: Paul Atterbury and Louise Irvine, *Gilbert Bayes Sculptor 1872–1953* (Richard Dennis, 1998), p.172

196                197

**198**

BENHAM AND FROUD
LONDON [MANUFACTURER]
*Purdonium*, the design registered 1892

Brass and wrought iron, stamped to rim *RD. 185979*
23 inches (58.4 cm)
LITERATURE: cf. Noël Riley, *The Elements of Design* (Mitchell Beazley, 2003), p.268, for an example with shovel

**199**

WILLIAM ARTHUR SMITH BENSON
1854–1924 [DESIGNER]
W.A.S. BENSON AND CO., HAMMERSMITH, LONDON
[MANUFACTURER]
*Chafing dish, c.1900*

Brass and copper, underside stamped *w.a.s. | benson* ['c' type]
9 inches (22.9 cm)
LITERATURE: Ian Hamerton (editor), *W.A.S. Benson* (Antique Collectors' Club, 2005) p.86 plate 59

**200**

WILLIAM ARTHUR SMITH BENSON
1854–1924 [DESIGNER]
W.A.S. BENSON AND CO., HAMMERSMITH, LONDON
[MANUFACTURER]
*Table lamp, c.1900*

Brass and copper, stamped *w.a.s. | benson* ['c' type]
15 inches (38.1 cm) high to gallery
LITERATURE: cf. Ian Hamerton (editor), *W.A.S. Benson* (Antique Collectors' Club, 2005) p.248 pl. 3

**201**

WILLIAM ARTHUR SMITH BENSON
1854–1924 [DESIGNER]
W.A.S. BENSON AND CO., HAMMERSMITH, LONDON
[MANUFACTURER]
*Pair of candlesticks, c.1900*

Cast and weighted bronze with copper bobeche, the candle-holders each stamped *w.a.s. | benson* ['c' type]
4¼ inches (10.8 cm) high, 13½ inches (34.3 cm) long
LITERATURE: cf. Ian Hamerton (editor), *W.A.S. Benson* (Antique Collectors' Club, 2005) p.120 pl.96

## 202

WILLIAM ARTHUR SMITH BENSON
1854–1924 [DESIGNER]
W.A.S. BENSON AND CO., HAMMERSMITH, LONDON
[MANUFACTURER]

*Banner holder, c.1900*

Brass with traces of copper plating, the underside of foot stamped
*W.A.S. | BENSON* ['C' type]
8 inches (20.3 cm) high, 16¼ inches (41.3 cm) long
LITERATURE: cf. Ian Hamerton (editor), *W.A.S. Benson* (Antique
Collectors' Club, 2005) p.121 plate 98

## 203

WILLIAM ARTHUR SMITH BENSON
1854–1924 [DESIGNER]
W.A.S. BENSON AND CO., HAMMERSMITH, LONDON
[MANUFACTURER]

*Counter-weighted lamp, c.1900*

Cast and weighted bronze with brass shade
9⅜ inches (23.8 cm) high, 16 inches (40.6 cm) long
LITERATURE: cf. Ian Hamerton (editor), *W.A.S. Benson* (Antique
Collectors' Club, 2005) p.120 pl. 96 and p.257 pl. 8 (927/s)

## 204

WILLIAM ARTHUR SMITH BENSON
1854–1924 [DESIGNER]
W.A.S. BENSON AND CO., HAMMERSMITH, LONDON
[MANUFACTURER]

*Dutch oven, c.1900*

Copper and iron · 23½ × 14¾ × 11½ inches (59.7 × 37.5 × 29.2 cm)
LITERATURE: *Price List of Fittings for Oil, Gas, Candle Table Ware,
etc.* (W.A.S. Benson and Co., London, 1899–1900), plate 29, no. 774;

cf. Ian Hamerton, editor, *W.A.S. Benson* (Antique Collectors'
Club, 2005) p.98 plate 76 and p.99 plate 77

## 205

CHARLES BEVAN
FL. 1865–83 [DESIGNER]
GILLOWS, LANCASTER [MANUFACTURER]

*'New Registered Reclining Chair', first advertised 1865*

Oak with brass fittings and replacement upholstery, the underside
stamped *GILLOWS · LANCASTER*
35½ × 25½ × 34½ inches (90.2 × 64.8 × 87.6 cm) upright; 44 inches
long (111.8 cm) extended
LITERATURE: cf. Jeremy Cooper, *Victorian and Edwardian Furniture
and Interiors* (London, 1987), fig.267

## 206

CHARLES BEVAN
FL. 1865–83 [DESIGNER]

*'New Registered Reclining Chair', first advertised 1865*

Mahogany with ebonized wood, brass fittings and castors, and
replacement deep-buttoned leather
36½ × 25½ × 32¾ inches (92.7 × 64.8 × 83.2 cm) upright; 44 inches
(111.8 cm) long extended
LITERATURE: cf. Jeremy Cooper, *Victorian and Edwardian Furniture
and Interiors* (London, 1987), fig.267

## 207

C. H. BRANNAM LTD
BARNSTAPLE, DEVON [MANUFACTURER]

*Cache pot, 1900*

Base incised *C H Brannam | Barum | 1900 | BW*
6¾ inches (17.1 cm)

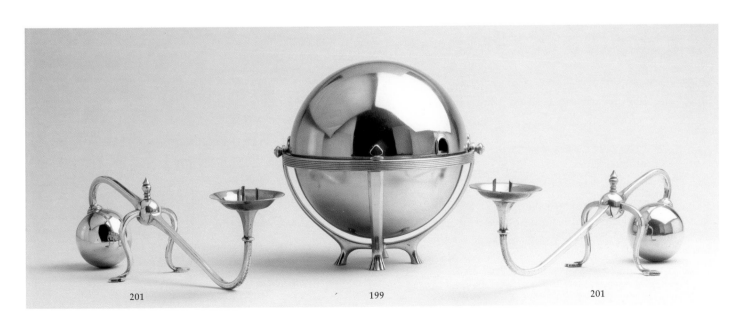

201                    199                    201

208

C. H. BRANNAM LTD
BARNSTAPLE, DEVON [MANUFACTURER]

*Galleon*, the design registered 1886

Incised on side, Rd. 44561, base incised *C H Brannam | Barum | 1900 | BW* · 8⅛ inches (20.6 cm) high, 12 inches (30.5 cm) long
PROVENANCE: Charles and Lavinia Handley-Read

209

BURMANTOFTS [WILCOX AND CO.]
LEEDS [MANUFACTURER]

*Vase*, 1882–1904, probably before 1891

Base impressed with manufacturer's monogram | *B* | *106* [shape number] · 11½ inches (29.2 cm)

210

BURMANTOFTS [WILCOX AND CO.]
LEEDS [MANUFACTURER]

*Vase*, 1882–1904, probably before 1891

Base impressed with manufacturer's monogram | *1450* | incised *EB*
20¼ inches (51.4 cm)
EXHIBITED: The Fine Art Society, *The Aesthetic Movement and the Cult of Japan*, 1972 (91)
LITERATURE: The Fine Art Society, *The Aesthetic Movement and the Cult of Japan*, exhibition catalogue (London, 1972), p.23 cat.91.

211

BURMANTOFTS [WILCOX AND CO.]
LEEDS [MANUFACTURER]

*Vase*, 1891–1904

Base impressed with manufacturer's monogram | *ENGLAND* | *106* [shape number] and bearing label written by Charles Handley-Read: *from Monica | Anthony, Porto- | bello Rd. Feb | 1969 £5.10.0*
11¼ inches (28.6 cm)
PROVENANCE: Monica Anthony; Charles Handley-Read
EXHIBITED: The Fine Art Society, *The Aesthetic Movement and the Cult of Japan*, 1972 (94)
LITERATURE: The Fine Art Society, *The Aesthetic Movement and the Cult of Japan*, exhibition catalogue (London, 1972), p.23 cat.94

212

BURMANTOFTS [WILCOX AND CO.]
LEEDS [MANUFACTURER]

*Vase*, 1882–1904, probably before 1891

Base impressed with manufacturer's monogram | *434* [shape number] | incised signature *EB*, and bearing labels written by Charles Handley-Read: *Portobello Rd | July 13 1968 | £9.0.0 – | too much!*
10½ inches (26.7 cm)
PROVENANCE: Charles and Lavinia Handley-Read
EXHIBITED: The Fine Art Society, *The Aesthetic Movement and the Cult of Japan*, 1972 (92)

LITERATURE: The Fine Art Society, *The Aesthetic Movement and the Cult of Japan*, exhibition catalogue (London, 1972), p.23 cat.92.

213

BURMANTOFTS [WILCOX AND CO.]
LEEDS [MANUFACTURER]

*Vase*, 1882–1904, probably before 1891

Base impressed with manufacturer's monogram | incised *B* | painted *TWL*
4⅜ inches (11.1 cm)

214

BURMANTOFTS [WILCOX AND CO.]
LEEDS [MANUFACTURER]

*Crouching toad*, 1891–1904

Base impressed with manufacturer's monogram | *ENGLAND* | *1897* | *T*
5¾ inches (14.6 cm)

215

BURMANTOFTS [WILCOX AND CO.]
LEEDS [MANUFACTURER]

*Crouching toad*, 1891–1904

Base impressed with manufacturer's monogram | *ENGLAND* | *1897*
5¾ inches (14.6 cm)

216

BURMANTOFTS [WILCOX AND CO.]
LEEDS [MANUFACTURER]

*Toad*, 1891–1904

Base impressed *BURMANTOFTS* | *FAIENCE* | *ENGLAND* | *583* | *T*
6⅜ inches (16.2 cm) high, 8 inches (20.3 cm) long

217

BURMANTOFTS [WILCOX AND CO.]
LEEDS [MANUFACTURER]

*Toad*, 1891–1904

Base impressed *BURMANTOFTS* | *FAIENCE* | *ENGLAND* | *583* | *T*
6⅜ inches (16.2 cm) high, 8 inches (20.3 cm) long

218

CRAVEN DUNNILL AND CO. LTD
JACKFIELD, SHROPSHIRE [MANUFACTURER]

*Four-tile panel*, c.1891

15½ × 11⅜ inches (39.4 × 28.9 cm)

219

CRAVEN DUNNILL AND CO. LTD
JACKFIELD, SHROPSHIRE [MANUFACTURER]

*Four-tile panel*, c.1891

15½ × 11⅜ inches (39.4 × 28.9 cm)

## 220

WILLIAM DE MORGAN
1839–1917 [DESIGNER]
WILLIAM DE MORGAN AND CO., LONDON [MANUFACTURER]

*'Rose and Scroll',* two tiles designed before 1888

Ruby lustre · Each tile 6 × 6 inches (15.2 × 15.2 cm)
LITERATURE: cf. Martin Greenwood, *The Designs of William De Morgan* (Dennis and Wiltshire, 1989), p.139 (665)

## 221

WILLIAM DE MORGAN
1839–1917 [DESIGNER]
WILLIAM DE MORGAN, MERTON ABBEY [MANUFACTURER]

*'Chicago' tile,* 1882–8

The iron base with cast mark: W DE MERTON | ABBEY | [Abbey device] · 9 inches (23 cm) square
LITERATURE: cf. Martin Greenwood, *The Designs of William De Morgan* (Dennis and Wiltshire, 1989), p.154 (563)

## 222

DR CHRISTOPHER DRESSER
1834–1904 [DESIGNER]
HENRY OGDEN AND SON, DEANSGATE, MANCHESTER [MANUFACTURER]

*Cabinet, c.1867*

Ebonized, incised, gilded and painted wood, the right door with incheset enamel plaque: MANUFACTURED BY | H. OGDEN & SON, | DEANSGATE MANCHESTER and stamped H. OGDEN | MANCHESTER | 5146, the lock stamped SAM & HALL | BIRMINGHAM
45⅛ × 30 × 14⅝ inches (114.6 × 76.2 × 37.1 cm)
EXHIBITED: London, Camden Arts Centre, and Middlesbrough, Dorman Museum, *Christopher Dresser,* 1979–80
LITERATURE: Harry Lyons, *Christopher Dresser: People's Designer, 1834–1904,* exhibition catalogue (New Century, 1999) np, fig.15

## 223

DR CHRISTOPHER DRESSER
1834–1904 [DESIGNER]
COALBROOKDALE CO., SHROPSHIRE [MANUFACTURER]

*Umbrella stand,* the design registered 1869

Cast iron, the reverse with cast registration lozenge for 29 September 1869, and *No. 42,* the removeable drip pan with cast mark: *No. 42–3*
32 × 19 × 6¾ inches (81.2 × 48.2 × 17.2 cm)
LITERATURE: *The Art Journal Catalogue of the International Exhibition* (1871), reproduced in Stuart Durant, *Christopher Dresser* (Academy Editions, 1993), p.100; *Furniture Gazette,* 1876, reproduced in Jeremy Cooper, *Victorian and Edwardian Furniture and Interiors* (London, 1987), fig.357

## 224

DR CHRISTOPHER DRESSER
1834–1904 [DESIGNER]
W. BOOTY, LONDON [MANUFACTURER]

*Side chair, c.1870*

Ebonized and gilt-incised wood and replacement antique Japanese upholstery
31⅞ × 17 × 17¾ inches (81 × 43.2 × 45.1 cm)
EXHIBITED: Fukushima, City Museum of Art; Tokyo, Fuchu Art Museum; Toyama, Takaoka City Museum of Art; Tochigi, Utsunomiya Museum of Art, *Christopher Dresser and Japan,* 2002 (173)
LITERATURE: *Christopher Dresser and Japan,* exhibition catalogue (Koriyama City Museum of Art, 2002) p.173 fig.173

1834–1904 [DESIGNER]
BENHAM AND FROUD, LONDON [MANUFACTURER]

*Coal shovel and tongs, c.1880*

Brass and wood, the shovel with indistinct manufacturer's stamp,
verso
The shovel 23⅜ inches (59.3 cm), the tongs 23¼ inches (59 cm)
LITERATURE: cf. Michael Whiteway, *Christopher Dresser 1834–1904*
(Skira, 2001), p.154 no. 181; Michael Whiteway, *Shock of the Old:
Christopher Dresser, Design Revolution* (London and New York,
2004), p.174 fig.235

## 226

DR CHRISTOPHER DRESSER
1834–1904 [DESIGNER]
JAMES W. AND C. WARD, HALIFAX [MANUFACTURER]

*Textile,* the design registered 1873

Silk damask
24 × 24 inches (61 × 61 cm)
LITERATURE: Stuart Durant, *Christopher Dresser* (Academy
Editions, 1993), p.52; cf. Michael Whiteway, *Shock of the Old:
Christopher Dresser, Design Revolution* (London and New York,
2004), p.75 fig 84, and Harry Lyons, *Christopher Dresser: The
People's Designer* (Antique Collectors' Club, 2005) p.240 plate 527

1834–1904 [DESIGNER]
JAMES W. AND C. WARD, HALIFAX [MANUFACTURER]

*Textile,* the design registered 1871

16¾ × 25½ inches (42.5 × 64.8 cm)
LITERATURE: Noël Riley, *The Elements of Design* (Mitchell Beazley,
2003), p.270; Harry Lyons, *Christopher Dresser: The People's
Designer* (Antique Collectors' Club, 2005) p.229 plate 480; cf.
Michael Whiteway, *Shock of the Old: Christopher Dresser, Design
Revolution* (London and New York, 2004), p.65 fig.60

An example of this textile was shown by Ward at the London
International Exhibition, 1871, reproduced in Whiteway, ibid, p.61

## 228

DR CHRISTOPHER DRESSER
1834–1904 [DESIGNER]
MINTON AND CO., STOKE-ON-TRENT [MANUFACTURER]

*Tile, c.1867*

Encaustic, impressed verso: MINTON & CO | PATENT | STOKE UPON
TRENT and indistinct date cipher
8 × 8 inches (20.3 × 20.3 cm)
LITERATURE: cf. Michael Whiteway, *Christopher Dresser 1834–1904*
(Skira, 2001), p.57 fig.15

**229**

DR CHRISTOPHER DRESSER
1834–1904 [DESIGNER]
MINTON AND CO., STOKE-ON-TRENT [MANUFACTURER]

*Soup bowl*, 1872

With printed manufacturer's marks and date cipher, verso
10 inches (25.4 cm) dia.

**230**

DR CHRISTOPHER DRESSER
1834–1904 [DESIGNER]
MINTON AND CO., STOKE-ON-TRENT [MANUFACTURER]

*Four tiles*, designed *c.1877*

Transfer-printed
Each tile 6 × 6 inches (15.2 × 15.2 cm) the panel 6 × 24 inches
(15.2 × 61 cm)
LITERATURE: cf. Stuart Durant, *Christopher Dresser* (Academy
Editions, 1993), p.109, and Michael Whiteway, *Shock of the Old:
Christopher Dresser, Design Revolution* (London and New York,
2004), p.84, fig.100

**231**

DR CHRISTOPHER DRESSER
1834–1904 [DESIGNER]
LINTHORPE ART POTTERY, MIDDLESBROUGH [MANUFACTURER]

*Vase*, 1879–89

2 inches (5.1 cm)

**232**

DR CHRISTOPHER DRESSER
1834–1904 [DESIGNER]
LINTHORPE ART POTTERY, MIDDLESBROUGH [MANUFACTURER]

*Vase with crimped rim*, *c.1879–89*

2¾ inches (7 cm)
LITERATURE: cf. *Christopher Dresser and Japan*, exhibition
catalogue (Koriyama City Museum of Art, 2002) p.109 fig.72

**233**

DR CHRISTOPHER DRESSER
1834–1904 [DESIGNER]
LINTHORPE ART POTTERY, MIDDLESBROUGH [MANUFACTURER]

*Vase*, 1879–82

Base impressed *340* | *LINTHORPE* | facsimile signature of
Christopher Dresser | raised monogram of Henry Tooth
10½ inches (26.7 cm)

**234**

DR CHRISTOPHER DRESSER
1834–1904 [DESIGNER]
LINTHORPE ART POTTERY, MIDDLESBROUGH [MANUFACTURER]

*Vase*, 1879–82

Base impressed *LINTHORPE* | facsimile signature of Christopher
Dresser | *114* | monogram of Henry Tooth
5¾ inches (14.6 cm)

**235**

DR CHRISTOPHER DRESSER
1834–1904 [DESIGNER]
LINTHORPE ART POTTERY, MIDDLESBROUGH [MANUFACTURER]

*Vase*, *c.1879–89*

2⅞ inches (7.3 cm)

**236**

DR CHRISTOPHER DRESSER
1834–1904 [DESIGNER]
LINTHORPE ART POTTERY, MIDDLESBROUGH [MANUFACTURER]

*Basket with handle*, 1879–82

Base impressed *LINTHORPE* | facsimile signature of Christopher
Dresser | *772* | monogram of Henry Tooth
4¾ inches (12.1 cm)
EXHIBITED: Milan, Palazzo della Triennale, *Christopher Dresser*,
2001–2
LITERATURE: Michael Whiteway, *Christopher Dresser 1834–1904*
(Skira, 2001), p.137 fig.149

**237**

DR CHRISTOPHER DRESSER
1834–1904 [DESIGNER]
LINTHORPE ART POTTERY, MIDDLESBROUGH [MANUFACTURER]

*Vase with double handle*, *c.1879–89*

Base impressed *LINTHORPE* | *596*
7⅞ inches (20 cm)
LITERATURE: Harry Lyons, *Christopher Dresser: The People's
Designer* (Antique Collectors' Club, 2005) p.92 plate 120 (left)

**238**

DR CHRISTOPHER DRESSER
1834–1904 [DESIGNER]
LINTHORPE ART POTTERY, MIDDLESBROUGH [MANUFACTURER]

*Conical vase*, *c.1879–82*

Base impressed *LINTHORPE* | facsimile signature of Christopher
Dresser | *HT* [monogram of Henry Tooth]
5¼ inches high (13.3 cm)
LITERATURE: Michael Whiteway, *Christopher Dresser 1834–1904*
(Skira, 2001), p.184 fig.226

**239**

DR CHRISTOPHER DRESSER
1834–1904 [DESIGNER]
LINTHORPE ART POTTERY, MIDDLESBROUGH [MANUFACTURER]

*Vase on three feet, c.1879–82*

Base impressed with facsimile signature of Christopher Dresser |
monogram of Henry Tooth | LINTHORPE
2½ inches (6.4 cm)

**240**

DR CHRISTOPHER DRESSER
1834–1904 [DESIGNER]
WATCOMBE POTTERY CO., ST MARY CHURCH [MANUFACTURER]

*Vase, c.1880*

The base impressed twice, WATCOMBE | TORQUAY | F88
5⅝ inches high (14.3 cm)
EXHIBITED: Milan, Palazzo della Triennale, *Christopher Dresser*,
2001–2
LITERATURE: Harry Lyons, *Christopher Dresser: People's Designer,
1834–1904*, exhibition catalogue (New Century, 1999) np, fig.40;
Michael Whiteway, *Christopher Dresser 1834–1904* (Skira, 2001),
p.72 fig.37

**241**

DR CHRISTOPHER DRESSER
1834–1904 [ATTRIBUTED DESIGNER]
WILLIAM AULT, SWADLINCOTE [MANUFACTURER]

*Wall vase, c.1895*

Base with moulded manufacturer's mark and impressed *346*
9 inches (23 cm)
LITERATURE: cf. *Pottery Gazette* (1 September 1896), reproduced in
Harry Lyons, *Christopher Dresser: The People's Designer* (Antique
Collectors' Club, 2005) p.82 plate 99

**242**

DR CHRISTOPHER DRESSER
1834–1904 [DESIGNER]
RICHARD PERRY, SON AND CO., WOLVERHAMPTON
[MANUFACTURER]

*Candlestick, c.1883*

Painted iron with moulded mark on underside, PERRY | SON | & CO
[in rope device] · 3¾ inches (9.5 cm) high × 7½ inches (19.1 cm)
long

**243**

DR CHRISTOPHER DRESSER
1834–1904 [DESIGNER]
RICHARD PERRY, SON AND CO., WOLVERHAMPTON
[MANUFACTURER]
JONES BROTHERS, PICCADILLY, LONDON [RETAILER]

*Candlestick and snuffer, c.1885*

Enamelled metal with printed stamp to underside, DR. DRESSER'S |
DESIGN and stamped label on underside: JONES BROS. |
IRONMONGERS | AND COPPERSMITHS | DOWN ST. PICCADILLY. W.
5 inches (12.7 cm) high, 8¾ inches (22.2 cm) long
EXHIBITED: Milan, Palazzo della Triennale, *Christopher Dresser*,
2001–2; New York, Cooper-Hewitt National Design Museum;
London, Victoria and Albert Museum, *Christopher Dresser 1834–
1904: A Design Revolution*, 2004
LITERATURE: Michael Whiteway, *Christopher Dresser 1834–1904*
(Skira, 2001), p.175 fig.212 (right); Michael Whiteway, *Shock of the
Old: Christopher Dresser, Design Revolution* (London and New
York, 2004), p.181, fig.245 (right); the design reproduced in Harry
Lyons, *Christopher Dresser: The People's Designer* (Antique
Collectors' Club, 2005) 224 plate 455

**244**

DR CHRISTOPHER DRESSER
1834–1904 [DESIGNER]
RICHARD PERRY, SON AND CO., WOLVERHAMPTON
[MANUFACTURER]

*'Kordofan' candlestick, the design registered 1883*

Enamelled metal, brass, wood, the brass handle mount stamped DR.
DRESSERS' [sic] | DESIGN. with registration mark for 30 October
1883, the underside with moulded mark of PERRY | SON | & CO. and
with painted registration mark for same date.
5⅝ inches (14.3 cm)
EXHIBITED: Milan, Palazzo della Triennale, *Christopher Dresser*,
2001–2; New York, Cooper-Hewitt National Design Museum;
London, Victoria and Albert Museum, *Christopher Dresser 1834–
1904: A Design Revolution*, 2004
LITERATURE: Michael Whiteway, *Christopher Dresser 1834–1904*
(Skira, 2001), p.175 fig.212 (left); Michael Whiteway, *Shock of the
Old: Christopher Dresser, Design Revolution* (London and New
York, 2004), p.181, fig.245 (left), the design reproduced in Harry
Lyons, *Christopher Dresser: The People's Designer* (Antique
Collectors' Club, 2005) p.223 plate 452

**245**

DUNMORE POTTERY, AIRTH, STIRLINGSHIRE
[MANUFACTURER]

*Vase, c.1880–1903*

Base impressed DUNMORE
14¾ inches (37.5 cm)

238

237

233

4

231

239

240

236

232

## 246

DUNMORE POTTERY, AIRTH, STIRLINGSHIRE
[MANUFACTURER]
*Toad, 1891–1903*

Underside impressed DUNMORE
6 inches (15.2 cm) high, 7 inches (17.8 cm) long

## 247

DUNMORE POTTERY, AIRTH, STIRLINGSHIRE
[ATTRIBUTED MANUFACTURER]
*Toad, c.1880–1903*

5¼ inches (13.3 cm)

## 248

DUNMORE POTTERY, AIRTH, STIRLINGSHIRE
[MANUFACTURER]
*Vase, c.1880–1903*

Base impressed DUNMORE
12½ in (31.8 cm)

## 249

DUNMORE POTTERY, AIRTH, STIRLINGSHIRE
[MANUFACTURER]
*Pair of 'Lady Dunmore Bowls', c.1880–1903*

Each impressed on underside, DUNMORE
4⅞ inches (12.4 cm)

The design of this bowl recalls the work of the Scottish architect
Alexander 'Greek' Thomson 1817–75; they were named in honour
of Lady Catherine Dunmore

## 250

CHARLES LOCKE EASTLAKE
1836–1906 [DESIGNER]
JACKSON AND GRAHAM, LONDON [MANUFACTURER]
*Drawing-Room Sofa, c.1874*

Oak with carved decoration, padded back panel, and replacement
upholstery
34¾ × 71½ × 26⅝ inches (88.3 × 181.6 × 67.6 cm)
LITERATURE: Charles Locke Eastlake, *Hints on Household Taste in
Furniture, Upholstery and Other Details* (fourth edition, London,
1878), p.167 plate XXIV, in which the sofa has a carved date of 1874

## 251

COL. SIR ROBERT WILLIAM EDIS
1839–1927 [DESIGNER]

*Side chair*, designed c.1881

Carved and turned wood with spindled back-rest and upholstered seat · 32 × 18 × 20¼ inches (81.3 × 45.7 × 51.4 cm)
LITERATURE: cf. Robert Edis, *Decoration and Furniture of Town Houses* (London, 1881), frontispiece; an engraving of the chair in Jackson and Graham's bedroom at the International Health Exhibition, 1884, illustrated in Mark Girouard, *Sweetness and Light* (Oxford, 1977) p.135 plate 122
An example of this design was shown at the Health Exhibition held in London in 1884

## 252

ELKINGTON AND CO., BIRMINGHAM
[MANUFACTURER]

*Knife, c.1880*

Engraved silver-plated metal with cloisonné handle, stamped *E & Co. Y | E & Co.* [in shield below crown]

## 253

GLASGOW SCHOOL,
ATTRIBUTED TO TALWIN MORRIS
1865–1911

*Vase, c.1905*

Repoussé brass · 7⅛ inches (18 cm)

## 254

EDWARD WILLIAM GODWIN
1833–86 [DESIGNER]

*Side table*, designed c.1867

Ebonised wood with japanned decoration
27⅞ × 16 × 15¾ inches (70.8 × 40.6 × 40 cm)

## 255

EDWARD WILLIAM GODWIN
1833–86 [DESIGNER]
WILLIAM WATT, LONDON [ATTRIBUTED MANUFACTURER]

*Side chair*, designed in 1869

35¼ × 16½ × 18 inches (90.2 × 41.9 × 45.7 cm)
PROVENANCE: Elizabeth Aslin
LITERATURE: *Art Furniture*, trade catalogue (William Watt, 1877), plates 2 and 8; cf. Elizabeth Aslin, *E. W. Godwin: Furniture and Interior Decoration*, exhibition catalogue (The Fine Art Society, 1986), p.26 (8), illus p.42.

## 256

EDWARD WILLIAM GODWIN
1833–86 [ATTRIBUTED DESIGNER]

*Stand, c.1875*

Ebonized and gilded wood, the base stamped 5479
27¾ inches high (70.5 cm)
EXHIBITED: The Fine Art Society, *Whistler and Godwin*, 2001 (60)
LITERATURE: The Fine Art Society, *Whistler and Godwin*, exhibition catalogue (2001) p.78 no.60.

## 257

EDWARD WILLIAM GODWIN
1833–86 [DESIGNER]

*Side table*, designed c.1867

Gilt-incised wood with japanned decoration
27⅞ × 16 × 15¾ inches (70.8 × 40.6 × 40 cm)

256

## 258

EDWARD WILLIAM GODWIN
1833–86 [DESIGNER]

*Side table*, designed c.1867

Gilt-incised wood, veneered with amboyna and other woods
27 × 15⅞ × 16 (68.6 × 40.5 × 40.7 cm)

## 259

EDWARD WILLIAM GODWIN
1833–86 [DESIGNER]

*Side table*, designed c.1867

Ebonized and gilded wood, with folding flaps
26 × 16¾ × 16¾ (66 × 42.5 × 42.5 cm; 29¼ inches (74.3 cm) with flaps

## 260

EDWARD WILLIAM GODWIN
1833–86 [DESIGNER]
COLLINSON AND LOCK, LONDON [MANUFACTURER]

*Centre table*, c.1872–5

Mahogany
29 × 41 × 42 inches (73.5 × 104 × 106.8 cm)
EXHIBITED: The Fine Art Society, *Whistler and Godwin*, 2001 (47)
LITERATURE: Lionel Lambourne, *Aesthetic Movement* (Phaidon
Press, London, 1996) p.159; Susan Weber Soros, *The Secular
Furniture of E. W. Godwin* (New York, 1999), p.150 no.214; The Fine
Art Society, *Whistler and Godwin*, exhibition catalogue (2001), p.70
no.47

Presented to Andrew McIntosh Patrick on the occasion of his sixtieth
birthday, 1994

## 261

EDWARD WILLIAM GODWIN
1833–86 [DESIGNER]
HOLLAND AND SONS, LONDON [MANUFACTURER]

*Table*, based on a c.1869 design

Ebonized wood · 27¼ × 29⅞ × 17¾ inches (69.2 × 76 × 45.1 cm)
PROVENANCE: Charles Handley-Read

## 262

GOTHIC REVIVAL

*Stool*, c.1870

Carved and turned mahogany with incised decoration and buttoned
leather upholstered seat
20¾ × 19¼ × 15¾ inches (52.7 × 52.7 × 40 cm)
PROVENANCE: Charles and Lavinia Handley-Read
EXHIBITED: London, Royal Academy of Arts, *Victorian and
Edwardian Decorative Art: The Handley-Read Collection*, March-
April 1972 (B22)
LITERATURE: *Victorian and Edwardian Decorative Art: The Handley-
Read Collection*, exhibition catalogue (London, 1972), p.27 (cat.B22)

## 263

KATE GREENAWAY
1846–1901 [DESIGNER]

*Cabinet*, c.1886

Stained oak, brass mounts and glass, inscribed on label, verso: *Miss
Kate Greenaway | designed this Cabinet | for us. F.L.L.* <u>1886</u>
60⅞ × 37¼ × 14¼ inches (154.5 × 94.6 × 36.2 cm)
PROVENANCE: Frederick Locker-Lampson (1821–95); Sotheby's,
London, 23 June 1970 (lot 152)

Frederick Locker-Lampson, was a poet and mentor of the young Kate
Greenaway. He took an interest in Greenaway's career and
introduced her to society; she was flattered by his attentions and
although she was shy, Locker-Lampson took her to museums, social
events and introduced her to society in general. This cabinet was
kept together with a portrait of Locker-Lampson by Greenaway until
the portrait was sold at the same sale as the cabinet (lot 102).

## 264

GREGORY AND CO., LONDON [MANUFACTURER]

*Music cabinet*, c.1875

Carved and ebonized wood with incised and part-ebonized panels of
contrasting wood, bronze hinges, escutcheon and castors, mirror
glass, the right door stamped *GREGORY & CO. | 212 & 214 REGENT
STREET | LONDON | 1024*
48½ × 18¼ × 13¾ inches (123.2 × 46.4 × 34.9 cm)

## 265

GREGORY AND CO., LONDON
[ATTRIBUTED MANUFACTURER]

*Fire screen*, c.1875

Gilded, silvered and painted mahogany, painted on underside *217*.
40⅞ × 26 × 11⅛ inches (103.8 × 66 × 28.2 cm)

## 266

CHARLES HINDLEY AND SONS, LONDON
[MANUFACTURER]

*Music Cabinet*, c.1875

Mahogany with bronze hinges, escutcheon and castors, the interior
with three moveable shelves, the left door stamped *8879 C. HINDLEY
& SONS | OXFORD STREET LONDON*
48¾ × 18¼ × 12½ inches (123.8 × 46.4 × 31.8 cm)

## 267

GEORGE WASHINGTON JACK
1855–1932
MORRIS AND CO., LONDON [MANUFACTURER]

*'Saville' armchair*, c.1890

Mahogany with brass castors and replacement upholstery
36½ × 27 × 28¾ inches (92.7 × 68.6 × 73 cm)

260

### 268

THOMAS JECKYLL
1827–1881 [DESIGNER]
ROBBINS AND COMPANY, DUDLEY [ATTRIBUTED
MANUFACTURER]

*Sconce*, the design registered 1875

Brass, with cast registration mark, verso, for 2 October 1875
19½ inches × 14½ × 4¼ inches (49.5 × 36.8 × 10.8 cm)
EXHIBITED: New York, The Bard Graduate Center, *Thomas Jeckyll:
Architect and Designer, 1827–1881* 2003 (139)
LITERATURE: Susan Weber Soros and Catherine Arbuthnott, *Thomas
Jeckyll: Architect and Designer, 1827–1881* (New York, 2003) p.235
and 263 (no. 139)

### 269

THOMAS JECKYLL
1827–1881 [DESIGNER]
BARNARD, BISHOP AND BARNARDS, NORWICH
[MANUFACTURER]

*Jardinière*, the design registered 1879

Brass and tin
8¼ × 21⅛ × 6¾ inches (21 × 53.6 × 17.2 cm)
EXHIBITED: London, Barbican Art Gallery; Tokyo, Setagaya Art
Museum, *Japan and Britain: An Aesthetic Dialogue 1850–1930*,
1991–2 (114); New York, The Bard Graduate Center, *Thomas Jeckyll:
Architect and Designer, 1827–1881* 2003 (142)
LITERATURE: Barnard, Bishop and Barnards, *Illustrated Catalogue*
(1878), no.855; "Stove Ornamentation", *Furniture Gazette* 13 (10
January 1880), p.23; "Messrs. Barnard, Bishop, and Barnard (of
Norwich) New Illustrated Catalogues", *Cabinet Maker* 1 (1 June
1881), p.188 and illus; Barnard, Bishop and Barnards, *Complete
Catalogue* (1884), p.338; Tomoko Sato and Toshio Watanabe, Eds,
*Japan and Britain: An Aesthetic Dialogue 1850–1930*, exhibition
catalogue, 1991 (Barbican Art Gallery), p.117 cat.114
Susan Weber Soros and Catherine Arbuthnott, *Thomas Jeckyll:
Architect and Designer, 1827–1881* (New York, 2003) p.223 and 263
(no. 142)

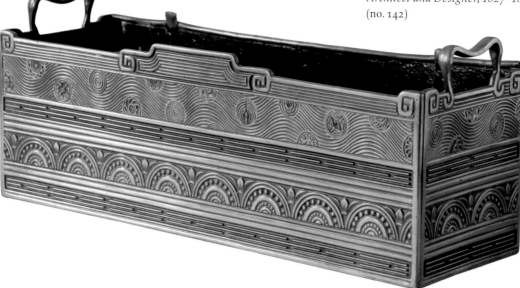

## 270

THOMAS JECKYLL
1827–1881 [DESIGNER]
BARNARD, BISHOP AND BARNARDS, NORWICH
[MANUFACTURER]

*Fender,* the design registered 1875

Cast and pierced brass, the back stamped three times *4 | 0* and with
two registration marks for 23 December 1875
7¼ × 48 × 11¾ inches (18.4 × 121.9 × 29.8 cm)
EXHIBITED: New York, The Bard Graduate Center, *Thomas Jeckyll:
Architect and Designer, 1827–1881* 2003 (137)
LITERATURE: Barnard, Bishop and Barnards, *Illustrated Catalogue*
(1878) p.331; idem, *Complete Catalogue* (1884); Susan Weber Soros
and Catherine Arbuthnott, *Thomas Jeckyll: Architect and Designer,
1827–1881* (New York, 2003), p.222 (fig.6–57) and 262 (no. 137)

## 271

THOMAS JECKYLL
1827–1881 [DESIGNER]
BARNARD, BISHOP AND BARNARDS, NORWICH
[MANUFACTURER]

*Ashes pan,* the design registered 1876

Brass, stamped *18 IN | 850,* with registration mark for 20 June 1876,
and brass reflectors
3⅜ × 18½ × 4¾ inches (8.6 × 47 × 12.1 cm)
LITERATURE: cf. Susan Weber Soros and Catherine Arbuthnott,
*Thomas Jeckyll: Architect and Designer, 1827–1881* (New York,
2003) p.222 figs 6–58 and 6–59

## 272

THOMAS JECKYLL
1827–1881 [DESIGNER]
BARNARD, BISHOP AND BARNARDS, NORWICH
[MANUFACTURER]

*Plaque, c.1879*

Brass · 18¼ × 8¾ inches (46.4 × 22.2 cm)
LITERATURE: cf. "Stove Ornamentation", *Furniture Gazette* 13 (10
January 1880), p.23, where a similar plaque is shown incorporated
in a stove front

## 273

THOMAS JECKYLL
1827–1881 [DESIGNER]
BARNARD, BISHOP AND BARNARDS, NORWICH
[MANUFACTURER]

*Plaque, c.1879*

Brass
15 × 8¾ inches (38 × 22.2 cm)
LITERATURE: cf. "Stove Ornamentation", *Furniture Gazette* 13 (10
January 1880), p.23, where a similar plaque is shown incorporated
in a stove front

## 274

OWEN JONES
1809–74 [DESIGNER]
WARNER, SILLETT AND RAMM [MANUFACTURER]

*'Sutherland',* designed *c.*1872

Jacquard Woven Silk · 16½ × 17 inches (42 × 43 cm)
LITERATURE: cf. The Fine Art Society, *Arts and Crafts Textiles,*
exhibition catalogue (1999) Cat.7; Linda Parry, *The Victoria and
Albert Museum's Textile Collection: British Textiles from 1850*
(London, 1993), p.58 plate 66

*Illustrated on inside cover*

## 275

LIBERTY AND CO., LONDON
[ATTRIBUTED RETAILER]

*'Thebes' chair,* based on a design registered in 1884

Walnut with cord · 23⅛ × 14¾ × 16¾ inches (58.7 × 37.5 × 42.5 cm)

## 276

LIBERTY AND CO., LONDON
[ATTRIBUTED RETAILER]

*'Thebes' stool,* based on a design registered in 1884

Mahogany
14¾ × 14 × 12⅜ inches (37.5 × 35.6 × 31.5 cm)
LITERATURE: cf. Jeremy Cooper, *Victorian and Edwardian Furniture
and Interiors* (London, 1987), fig.664

## 277

LINTHORPE ART POTTERY, MIDDLESBROUGH
[ATTRIBUTED MANUFACTURER]

*Cluster vase, c.1879–89*

6⅛ inches (15.6 cm)

## 278

LINTHORPE ART POTTERY, MIDDLESBROUGH
[MANUFACTURER]

*Wall bracket,* 1879–89

The back impressed *LINTHORPE* (in vase device) *| 1739* and with
painted accession number *ART.NOUV. | 1933 | A 2*
16¼ × 13½ × 6½ inches (41.3 × 34.3 × 16.5 cm)
Showing the strong influence of Dr Christopher Dresser

## 279

LINTHORPE ART POTTERY, MIDDLESBROUGH
[MANUFACTURER]

*Wall vase, c.1879–89*

Reverse impressed *LINTHORPE* (in vase device) *| 1708* and with
painted accession number *ART.NOUV. | 1933 | A 2*
11½ × 13¼ × 3⅛ inches (29.2 × 33.7 × 8 cm)
Showing the strong influence of Dr Christopher Dresser

278

279

## 280

ROBERT WALLACE MARTIN
1843–1923 [MAKER]
MARTIN BROTHERS, LONDON [MANUFACTURER]

*Vase*, 1875

Inscribed around the neck: *R W Martin – London – 1875*, the base incised *D.46.* | *R W Martin* | *London* | *2–1875* · 12½ inches (31.8 cm)
PROVENANCE: Charles and Lavinia Handley-Read
EXHIBITED: The Fine Art Society, *The Aesthetic Movement and the Cult of Japan*, 1972 (134)
LITERATURE: The Fine Art Society, *The Aesthetic Movement and the Cult of Japan*, exhibition catalogue (London, 1972), p.26 cat.134 (illus.)

## 281

ROBERT WALLACE MARTIN
1843–1923 [MAKER]
MARTIN BROTHERS, LONDON AND SOUTHALL
[MANUFACTURER]

*Vase*, 1880

The base incised *R W Martin* | *London &* | *Southall* | *572* | *21.4.80*
8⅝ inches (22 cm)
PROVENANCE: Charles and Lavinia Handley-Read

## 282

MARTIN BROTHERS, LONDON AND SOUTHALL
[MANUFACTURER]

*Vase and cover*, 1883

Base incised *Martin Bros* | *London & Southall* | *1–83*
9 inches (23 cm)

## 283

MARTIN BROTHERS, LONDON AND SOUTHALL
[MANUFACTURER]

*Vase*, 1911

The base incised *6–1911* | *Martin Bros – London & Southall*
11 inches (28 cm)

## 284

MARTIN BROTHERS, LONDON AND SOUTHALL
[MANUFACTURER]

*Vase*, 1903

Base incised *8–1903* | *Martin Bros* | *London & Southall*
8¾ inches (22.2 cm)

## 285

MARTIN BROTHERS, SOUTHALL [MANUFACTURER]

*Jardiniere*, the design registered 1908

Base incised *Rd. 544322* | *Southall* | *Potteries*
8 inches (20.3 cm)

## 286

MINTON AND CO., STOKE-ON-TRENT
[MANUFACTURER]

*Cluster vase*, 1876

Base impressed *MINTONS* | *193* | *D* | Date cipher for 1876
5¼ inches (13.3 cm)

## 287

MINTON AND CO., STOKE-ON-TRENT
[MANUFACTURER]

*Raised dish*, 1862

Gilded ceramic, the underside impressed *MINTON* | date cipher for 1862 · 2½ inches (6.4 cm) high, 5 inches (12.7 cm) dia.
PROVENANCE: Charles and Lavinia Handley-Read

## 288

SAMUEL MOORE AND SON, LONGTON
[MANUFACTURER]

*Vase*, 1868–75

*Pâte-sur-pâte*, gilded and painted decoration, the base impressed *MOORE* · 5 inches (12.7 cm)
LITERATURE: Noël Riley, *The Elements of Design* (Mitchell Beazley, 2003), p.263

## 289

BERNARD MOORE
1850–1935

*Covered jar*, 1905–1915

The lid with unknown monogram, the underside of lid and base marked *BERNARD* | *MOORE*, the base impressed *1175*
6¾ inches (17 cm)

## 290

WILLIAM STAITE MURRAY
1881–1962

*Vase*, 1922

Base incised *W. S. Murray* | *9* | *1922* | *London* · 4⅞ inches (12.4 cm)

## 291

WILLIAM JAMES NEATBY
1860–1910

*Plaque*, 1887

Signed and dated verso, *WM. J NEATBY* | *1887* | *P.G.*
12⅜ inches. (31.5 cm) dia.
EXHIBITED: London, Barbican Art Gallery; Tokyo, Setagaya Art Museum, *Japan and Britain: An Aesthetic Dialogue 1850–1930*, 1991–2 (201,190)
LITERATURE: Tomoko Sato and Toshio Watanabe, editors, *Japan and Britain: An Aesthetic Dialogue 1850–1930*, exhibition catalogue, 1991 (Barbican Art Gallery), cat.201 p.130 (Japanese edition), cat.190, p.133, illus.

## 292

MAW AND CO., JACKFIELD, SALOP [MANUFACTURER]

*Koto player, c.1880–90*

Transfer-printed on two tiles, each impressed with manufacturer's device, *FLOREAT MAW SALOPIA | MAW & CO | BENTHALL WORKS | JACKFIELD | SALOP*
6 × 12 inches (15.2 × 30.5 cm)

## 293

DANIEL PABST, PHILADELPHIA
1826–1910
[ATTRIBUTED DESIGNER]

*Hanging cabinet, c.1880*

Carved walnut with engraved brass strap-hinges
45 × 30½ × 11 inches (114.3 × 77.5 × 27.9 cm)

## 294

PILKINGTON'S TILE AND POTTERY CO. LTD,
CLIFTON JUNCTION [MANUFACTURER]
GLADYS M. RODGERS, ACTIVE 1907–28 [DECORATOR]

*Covered jar, 1914–19*

Gold lustre, the base with painted monogram of artist, and impressed with manufacturer's cipher | *ROYAL LANCASTRIAN | ENGLAND*
9½ inches (24.1 cm)
LITERATURE: cf. Malcolm Haslam, *English Art Pottery 1865–1915* (Antique Collectors' Club, 1975), pl. 152

## 295

PILKINGTON'S TILE AND POTTERY CO. LTD,
CLIFTON JUNCTION [MANUFACTURER]
W. S. MYCOCK, ACTIVE 1906–38 [DECORATOR]

*Covered Jar, 1919*

Base painted with artist's monogram, dated 1919, and impressed with manufacturer's cipher | *ROYAL LANCASTRIAN | ENGLAND*
5¼ inches (13.3 cm)

## 296

PILKINGTON'S TILE AND POTTERY CO. LTD,
CLIFTON JUNCTION [MANUFACTURER]
GORDON M. FORSYTH 1879–1952 [DECORATOR]

*Cup with two handles, 1908*

Gold and ruby lustre, inscribed *QVI NON LABORAT | NON MANDUCET* (He who does not work will not eat), the base painted with a leaping gazelle and artist's monogram, impressed with manufacturer's cipher | *VIII | ENGLAND | 2793 · 9¼* inches (23.5 cm)
PROVENANCE: Richard Dennis; Charles and Lavinia Handley-Read
EXHIBITED: London, Royal Academy of Arts, *Victorian and Edwardian Decorative Art: The Handley-Read Collection*, 1972 (G37)
LITERATURE: *Victorian and Edwardian Decorative Art: The Handley-Read Collection*, exhibition catalogue (London, 1972), p.120 cat.G37; cf. A. J. Cross, *Pilkington's Royal Lancastrian Pottery and Tiles* (Richard Dennis, 1980), p.53 plate 66

'Charles Handley-Read state in one of the notes left by his deathbed that Lavinia would let Andrew McIntosh Patrick choose a "Pilk". T. Stainton kindly allowed me to choose this. My choice was swayed by the Calvanistic inscription'.

## 297

PILKINGTON'S TILE AND POTTERY CO. LTD,
CLIFTON JUNCTION [MANUFACTURER]
RICHARD JOYCE [DECORATOR]

*Vase, 1908*

Gold and ruby lustre, the base painted with a stag | artist's monogram | impressed with manufacturer's cipher | *VIII | ENGLAND | 2620*
6¾ inches (17.1 cm)

296

297

294

289

295

## 298

JAMES POWELL, WHITEFRIARS [MANUFACTURER]

*Vase, 1870–1910*

Opalescent glass · 6½ inches (16.5 cm)

LITERATURE: cf. Wendy Evans et al, *Whitefriars Glass: James Powell and Sons of London* (London, 1995), p.60 fig.56, and Leslie Jackson, ed, Whitefriars Glass (1996) p.100 pl. 16 (iii)

## 299

AUGUSTUS WELBY NORTHMORE PUGIN
1812–52 [DESIGNER]

*Cabinet, c.1843*

Pine with iron escutcheons
54½ × 34½ × 16½ inches (138.4 × 87.6 × 41.9 cm)
PROVENANCE: A. W. N. Pugin, The Grange, Ramsgate, Kent

## 300

AUGUSTUS WELBY NORTHMORE PUGIN
1812–52 [DESIGNER]
MARSH, JONES AND CRIBB, LEEDS
[MANUFACTURER]

*Six side chairs, c.1870*

Walnut and replacement upholstery
34¾ × 18¾ × 20½ inches (88.3 × 47.6 × 52.1 cm)
LITERATURE: cf. Jeremy Cooper, *Victorian and Edwardian Furniture and Interiors* (London, 1987), fig.112

## 301

ROOKWOOD POTTERY, MOUNT ADAMS,
CINCINNATI [MANUFACTURER]

*Jug, 1903*

Base impressed with manufacturer's cipher | *III* | *259C.* | and incised *H.H.* (monogram) · 5¾ inches (14.6 cm)

## 302

ROOKWOOD POTTERY, MOUNT ADAMS,
CINCINNATI [MANUFACTURER]

*Vase, 1903*

Base impressed with manufacturer's cipher | *III* | *900D* | and incised *E.H.[N?]* · 6⅜ inches (16.2 cm)

## 303

M. AND H. SCHRENKEISEN, NEW YORK
CITY [MANUFACTURER]

*Rocking chair, c.1876*

Walnut with gilt incised decoration, the back stretcher with plaque: *SCHRENKEISEN'S ROCKER* | *PAT. OCT. 20. 1874* | *PAT. MAY. 23. 1876* | *N.Y.,* the side of inner frame stamped *19* | *33* · 36 × 24 × 30 inches (91.4 × 61 × 76.2 cm)

## 304

SMITH AND SON, DUNDEE [MANUFACTURER]
*Table, c.1880*

Carved and turned mahogany, with card on underside printed:
*SMITH & SON* | *Cabinet Makers* | *81, NETHERGATE* | *DUNDEE*
20 × 15½ inches dia. (50.8 × 39.4 cm)

## 305

ALFRED STEVENS 1817–75
*Maquettes for andiron finials, c.1852–3*

Plaster · 17 inches (43.2 cm)
PROVENANCE: By repute, commissioned by Robert Stainer Holford
for Dorchester House, Park Lane, London; Leicester Galleries,
London, after 1929
LITERATURE: *Art Journal Illustrated Catalogue of the International
Exhibition, London, 1862*, p.55; Susan Beattie, *Alfred Stevens, 1817–
75* (1975), p.10, and p.27, plate 23, design for a stove with male
figures for Hoole and Company

## 306

GODFREY SYKES
1824–66 [DESIGNER]

*Designs with figures for thirteen letters of the alphabet, 1864*

Pencil with black ink on paper, inscribed A.B.C. DONE BY | GODFREY SYKES | A.D. M DCCC LXIV
Each letter approx. 2¾ × 2¼ inches (7 × 5.7 cm)
PROVENANCE: Lord Clwyd; Charles and Lavinia Handley-Read
EXHIBITED: London, Royal Academy of Arts, *Victorian and Edwardian Decorative Art: The Handley-Read Collection*, 1972 (C90)
LITERATURE: *The South Kensington Museum, London: Examples of the Works of Art in the Museum and of Decorations of the Buildings*, part XII (1881–2), plate 89; *Building News*, 1885, p.280; *Victorian and Edwardian Decorative Art: The Handley-Read Collection*, exhibition catalogue (London, 1972), cat.C90, illus. p.59; cf. Charles Newton, *Victorian Designs for the Home* (Victoria and Albert Museum, 1999), pp.42–3.

Designs for the Centre Refreshment Room of the South Kensington Museum (now the Victoria and Albert Museum), which were executed in glazed earthenware by Minton, Hollins and Co. from 1867. They were used to form the inscription around the room: *There is nothing better for a man than that he should eat and drink and that he should make his soul good in his labour XYZ.*

## 307

GODFREY SYKES
1824–66 [DESIGNER]
MINTON, HOLLINS AND CO., [MANUFACTURER]

*Plaque, designed c.1864*

Glazed earthenware with painted mark, verso, *283 E*
12 × 10 inches (30.5 × 25.4 cm)

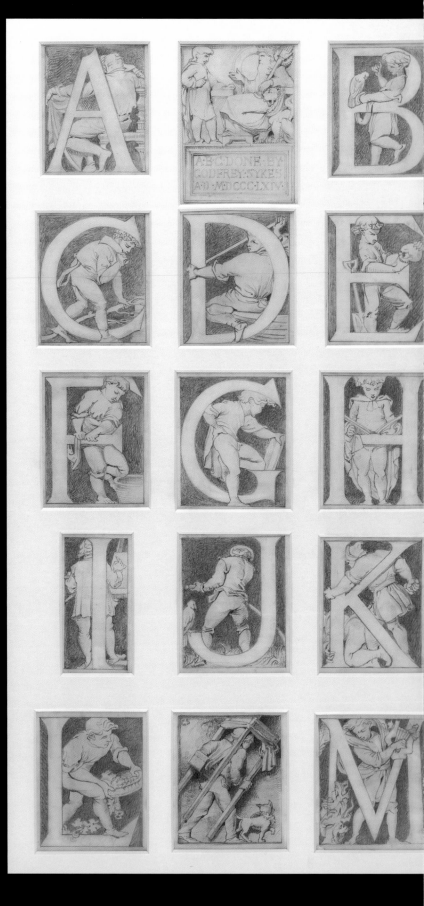

## 308

BRUCE JAMES TALBERT
1838–81 [DESIGNER]
PRATT AND PRINCE, BRADFORD [MANUFACTURER]

*Table, c.1876*

Ebonized, carved, turned and gilded wood inlaid with tropical woods, the underside with printed label, *PRATT & PRINCE,* | *Cabinet Makers and Upholsterers* | *CARPET AND BEDDING WAREHOUSEMEN* | *BRADFORD* · 27½ × 53½ × 29½ inches (70 × 136 × 75 cm)
LITERATURE: cf. Bruce James Talbert, *Examples of Ancient and Modern Furniture* (London, 1876), 'Old English' interior, with related settee

## 309

BRUCE JAMES TALBERT
1838–81 [DESIGNER]
PRATT AND PRINCE, BRADFORD [MANUFACTURER]

*Settee, c.1876*

Turned, carved and ebonized wood with gilded incised decoration, inlays and bands of wood, and brass castors.
32½ × 67¾ × 26½ inches (82.6 × 172 × 67.3 cm)
LITERATURE: cf. Bruce James Talbert, *Examples of Ancient and Modern Furniture*
(London, 1876),
'Old English' interior,
with related settee

## 310

TOOTH AND CO., BRETBY ART POTTERY, WOODVILLE
[MANUFACTURER]

*Stool, c.1891–1900*

Impressed with monogram of Henry Tooth | *BRETBY* | *ENGLAND* | C
13 inches (33 cm)

## 311

CHARLES VYSE
1882–1971

*Vase, 1945–63*

Base impressed C *VYSE* | *CHELSEA*
8⅝ inches (22 cm)

## 312

WATCOMBE POTTERY CO., ST MARY CHURCH

*Wall vase, c.1885–1901*

Reverse impressed with manufacturer's cipher, *WATCOMBE* | *SOUTH DEVON*
6½ inches (16.5 cm)

## 313

WEDGWOOD, ETRURIA
[ATTRIBUTED MANUFACTURER]

*Vase, c.1885*

The base with painted mark s *109 A* · 7⅛ inches (18.1 cm)

## 314

WEDGWOOD, ETRURIA [MANUFACTURER]
GEORGE A. MARSDEN [DESIGNER]

*Marsden ware vase, 1883*

Base impressed WEDGWOOD | L [date letter] and incised s.*193*
[pattern no.] · 10½ inches (26.7 cm)
LITERATURE: Maureen Batkin, *Wedgwood Ceramics 1846–1959*
(Richard Dennis, London, 1982) pp 109–10.

## 315

WHYTOCK AND REID, EDINBURGH
[MANUFACTURER]

*Table, c.1925*

Carved mahogany · 16¾ × 39 × 23¼ inches (42.5 × 99.1 × 59.1 cm)

## 316

WORCESTER ROYAL PORCELAIN CO., WORCESTER
[MANUFACTURER]

*Moon flask, 1878*

Transfer-printed, the base with impressed and printed
manufacturer's marks and date letter | *504* · 5¾ inches (14.6 cm)

## 317

WORCESTER ROYAL PORCELAIN CO., WORCESTER
[MANUFACTURER]

*Pair of candlesticks, 1875*

Hand-coloured and gilded transfer ware, the bases with impressed
and printed manufacturer's marks and date letter
6¾ inches (17.1 cm)

## 318

WORCESTER ROYAL PORCELAIN CO., WORCESTER
[MANUFACTURER]

*Double moon flask, 1878*

Transfer-printed, the base with impressed manufacturer's marks and
date letter | *504* · 5½ inches (14 cm)

## 319

WORCESTER ROYAL PORCELAIN CO., WORCESTER
[MANUFACTURER]

*Vase, 1878*

Hand-coloured and gilded transfer ware, the base with printed
manufacturer's marks and date letter · 4⅛ inches (10.5 cm)

## 320

ZSOLNAY, PECS
[ATTRIBUTED MANUFACTURER]

*Ornamental vase, c.1870*

Base impressed *1094* · 15⅛ inches (38.4 cm)

# The Andrew McIntosh Patrick Collection: The Twentieth Century

Further works from the collection of Andrew McIntosh Patrick will be included in our exhibition *The Twentieth Century*, 19 September to 11 October 2007. Enquiries: Annabel Thomas +44 (0)7816 680355

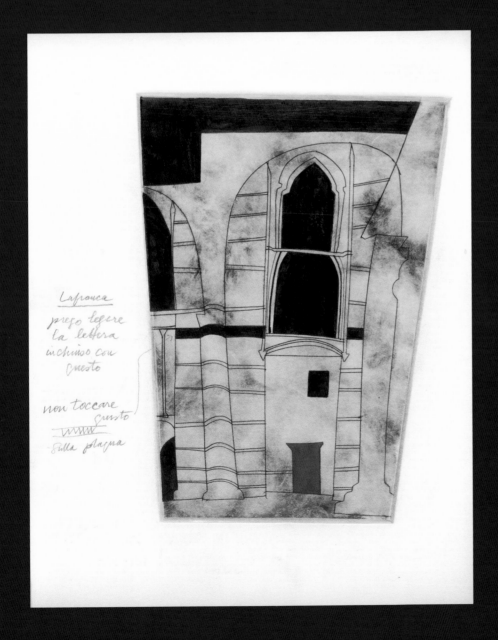

BEN NICHOLSON OM
1894–1982
*Siena, 1966*
Etching, extensively hand-coloured in gouache and black ink, inscribed in pencil by the artist
9⅝ × 7¼ inches
(24.5 × 18.3 cm)
PROVENANCE: François Lafranca

ACKNOWLEDGEMENTS

Many people have helped with the presentation of this
exhibition and we would like to thank Wendy Baron for her
perceptive and affectionate essay; Kenneth McConkey for
his research on the major Glasgow School paintings;
Christopher Forbes and Roger Billcliffe for hosting exhibitions
of selections from the collection in their galleries in New York
and Glasgow respectively; John McKenzie, Richard Holttum
and A. C. Cooper Ltd for photography; framers David Callanan
and Michael Callanan; restorers Michael Robinson, Philip
Robinson and Mary Goodwin; Robert Dalrymple for his
characteristically stylish design of the catalogue; and, of course,
to Andrew Patrick for making all this possible.
*Patrick Bourne*

Published by The Fine Art Society for the exhibition
*The Andrew McIntosh Patrick Collection*, 12 June to 5 July 2007
© All rights reserved

ISBN 978 0 905062 38 9

Designed and typeset in Aldus and Fairfield by Dalrymple
Photography by Richard Holttum, John McKenzie & A.C. Cooper Ltd
Printed in Belgium by Die Keure

Front cover: Sir John Lavery *Woman in Profile* (detail), 1883 [cat.94]

Frontispiece: Mariano Fortuny y Madrazo *A Marabou Stork* [cat.52]

Back cover: Dr Christopher Dresser (designer) Minton and Co.,
Stoke-on-Trent (manufacturer) *Tile c.*1867 [cat.228]

Inside covers: Owen Jones (designer) Warner, Sillett and Ramm
(manufacturer) *Sutherland textile*, designed *c.*1872 [cat.274]

Please contact Max Donnelly for condition reports on the
furniture and decorative arts: md@faslondon.com

DEALERS SINCE 1876

**FAS**

THE FINE ART
SOCIETY PLC